# The SOUTH LONDON Cook Book

A celebration of the amazing food & drink on our doorstep.
Featuring over 45 stunning recipes.

**The South London Cook Book**

©2017 Meze Publishing. All rights reserved.

First edition printed in 2017 in the UK.

**ISBN: 978-1-910863-27-5**

*Thank you to: José Pizarro, Adam Byatt*

*Compiled by: Will Savage*

*Written by: Kate Reeves-Brown, Aaron Jackson*

*Photography by: Xavier Buendia
(www.xdbphotography.com)*

*Additional photography: Mateo Orozco, Salt+Pickle*

*Edited by: Phil Turner*

*Designed by: Paul Cocker, Tom Crosby*

*PR: Kerre Chen*

*Contributors: Faye Bailey, Katie Fisher,
Sarah Koriba, Anna Tebble*

*Cover art: Luke Prest (www.lukeprest.com)*

me:ze
PUBLISHING

Published by Meze Publishing Limited
Unit 1b, 2 Kelham Square
Kelham Riverside
Sheffield S3 8SD
Web: www.mezepublishing.co.uk
Tel: 0114 275 7709
Email: info@mezepublishing.co.uk

Printed by Bell & Bain Ltd, Glasgow

# FOREWORD

Acclaimed Spanish chef José Pizarro made South London his home when he chose to open his first solo restaurant, José Tapas Bar on Bermondsey Street, followed by Pizarro just a few yards away.

I fell in love with South London when I was working at Borough Market, many years ago. I loved this area immediately… the people were always smiling and friendly, and the streets were so vibrant, they just buzzed with life. Borough Market reminded me of Spanish markets back home, full of amazing produce – the colours, the smells, the sights and the sounds were overwhelming for all the senses.

From co-founding Brindisa and Tapas Brindisa at Borough Market, to opening my first solo restaurant José Tapas Bar on Bermondsey Street, I have never ventured far away from this incredible foodie hub of creativity and passion. I love art, and this area is packed with artists, who add so much to the imaginative and innovative vibe of the community.

There are countless world-class restaurants serving every cuisine, and there are also sensational producers. I source amazing produce from a plethora of local suppliers – my butcher is nearby, my coffee supplier is local, I use fantastic London gin, an incredible baker and the most wonderful honey from Bermondsey Street Bees.

Throughout the time I've been part of the community here, I have watched as it has grown and developed, and I am proud to be a part of it. People make a community and the people here make it an inspiring place to run a business.

I hope you enjoy reading about the people and places that make up the food community of South London – and enjoy trying a few recipes, too!

*José Pizarro*

# FOREWORD

I first opened up shop in Clapham back in September 2001. I remember doing my research on the area, walking into M. Moens Butchers and seeing the most amazing produce. I thought, there has to be a market for a great restaurant here. Sixteen years later, and I'm still here cooking away, Trinity now has a Upstairs above it, a coveted Michelin Star and Bistro Union in Abbeville Village continues to provide for families and all day dining.

Clapham has changed beyond recognition and now has a fantastic food scene that seems to have given this little slice of South London a reputation all of its own. It's also thanks to Robin Gills' decision to open up here some years ago with his brilliant restaurant The Dairy that pushed things forward for us all.

There are now so many great places to eat at but, more importantly, to shop for great food. M. Moens continues to be a great source of organic and specialist meats and produce, and we now have The Ginger Pig in Abbeville Road, as well as Moxons, the most abundant fishmongers in Clapham South. Then there are the amazing ethnic markets and Indian restaurants to rival Brick Lane in Tooting, as well as Balham and its abundance of great all day eateries.

Venture south and Brixton has a reputation of its own for great food in the ever popular market and Pop Brixton, as well as some real foodie hotspots such as the brilliant Naughty Piglets. Moving into Peckham, you'll find vibrant markets and restaurants which are all about the food, try the Begging Bowl or Peckham Bazaar. There are many hidden gems in South London such as Silk Road in Peckham and Mien Tay in Battersea and, of course, the institution that is Chez Bruce in Wandsworth.

There's no shortage of pubs either, such as the Camberwell Arms and the famous Ship Inn on the river, and that's before you even get to Dulwich with its now vibrant and incredibly successful foodie destination Lordship Lane.

I still find it incredible how great food can bring about significant change to an area, great food brings with it a sense of pride in our community, a coming together to eat and share and of course the diversity that London is so famed for is more present in South London than almost anywhere else.

For me it's all about South London; I live here, cook here, eat here and am very proud to be a small part of this exciting Mecca for great food.

*Adam Byatt*

# CONTENTS

# *Deli* DELIGHTS

Celebrating five years since it opened its doors in Forest Hill,
Aga's Little Deli remains a treasure trove of gastronomic delights in the heart of
South-east London.

A sumptuous celebration of food, wine and music came together in autumn 2017 to mark the fifth birthday of Aga's Little Deli in Forest Hill. Aga opened her deli in September 2012, following many years working first at Neal's Yard and then Borough Market. Spending day after day surrounded by exquisite products inspired Aga to bring together under one roof a selection of the finest ingredients London has to offer.

Neal's Yard cheeses were an obvious choice for Aga, having worked at this famous London culinary institution. To this day, British cheeses are a speciality of the deli, alongside some lovely continental offerings. With charcuterie from Gastronomica, chorizo and other Spanish meats from Brindisa, there is a strong nod to Borough Market in this little shop. The fruits and vegetables come from Chegworth Valley in Kent, which ensures the local provenance and seasonality of the fresh groceries.

The café serves the best of what the deli has to offer in the form of freshly made sandwiches, salads and soups, complemented by coffee from the famous Monmouth Coffee, which is both served and sold on-site.

There is a sense of 'real food and drink' in everything at Aga's Little Deli, right down to the hot chocolate, which is made with luxurious real chocolate – no powder in sight!

A variety of gluten-free products is constantly expanding, alongside vegan cakes (the banana bread is a must-try) and some sugar-free goodies too. And even though Aga's is famous for its meats and cheeses, the range of vegan sandwiches is impressing the regulars too.

According to the owner, it is the customers who make Aga's Little Deli. She praises their loyalty over the last five years – many of whom she now counts as her close friends. She can even tell of a few deli love stories, which blossomed under her roof.

From one of the first little businesses to open in Forest Hill, Aga has watched the area thrive around her, and she looks forward to many more years in this charming little corner of South-east London.

# Aga's Little Deli

# BERMONDSEY FRIER ON SOURDOUGH

A British alternative to haloumi cheese served on sourdough bread with grilled tomato, homemade sweet and spicy chilli sauce, gherkins and rocket.

Preparation time: 5 minutes | Cooking time: 5-7 minutes | Serves 1-2

## Ingredients

100g Bermondsey Frier cheese

2 big slices fresh tomato

2 slices sourdough bread

A few gherkins

Rocket

Salt and pepper

**For the sweet and spicy chilli sauce:**

200g red chillies

2 big red peppers

2 sweet apples

2 tomato

1 white onion

400-500ml white wine vinegar

200g brown sugar

Olive oil, for frying

## Method

First make the sweet and spicy chilli sauce.

Slice the red chilli, red peppers, apples, tomato and onion, and fry them in a pan with a little olive oil for about 10 minutes, stirring it all the time. Don't allow it to burn. Add the white wine vinegar and brown sugar. Boil on a low heat for about 1-2 hours, adding water if needed throughout the cooking process, but not making it too watery. Blend the sauce and leave to cool. You can store the chilli sauce in the fridge for about 2 weeks.

Heat the frying pan or griddle pan – it needs to be really hot. Don't use any oil or butter, as the cheese is really fatty and rich as it is made from organic, full-fat milk. Season the cheese with salt, as it doesn't contain any salt; the only ingredients being milk and animal rennet. Cook the cheese on both sides in the hot pan until golden brown.

Grill the tomato slices at the same time, and toast the bread lightly.

Put three spoonfuls of the sweet and spicy sauce on both slices of the bread. Put some rocket and a few gherkins on top, followed by the cheese and grilled tomato. Season with salt and pepper, then enjoy!

# *Irresistibly* INDEPENDENT

A characterful pub full with a unique personality, The Alma holds a special place in the hearts of Crystal Palace locals.

From its previous guise as an iconic old live music venue, The Alma was lovingly restored when it was bought by Stephen Boyd in 2011. He carefully revealed the building's original character and restored the Victorian pub to a bright and airy space with huge windows and exposed brick walls. The jewel in the crown was the large garden at the back – a feature that was simply crying out to be given a new lease of life.

Stephen is passionate about independent pubs, having worked in the industry for his whole career. For him, the beauty of owning an independent pub means complete autonomy on choosing ethically sourced ingredients for the food, as well as wines from family-owned vineyards, and spirits and craft beers from small producers.

This is a view he shares with head chef James Browne who loves being able to devise his menus based on seasonal, local and ethically sourced ingredients direct from farmers and producers using the initiative Foodchain. From the breads to the sauces and stocks, every single thing is freshly made by hand in The Alma's own kitchen.

The huge garden is a special place tucked away in the centre of bustling Crystal Palace triangle. While it is the ideal place to enjoy a beer and BBQ in the sunshine in summer, it is just as suited to the cooler months when the covered and heated space is also bedecked with rugs to keep guests warm and cosy.

The Alma's garden is home to a fabulous Christmas fair each year, which sees 60 different local makers and producers showcase their products alongside Christmas tree-sellers in a wonderfully festive atmosphere.

True to its musical roots, The Alma is home to West End @ The Alma, a quarterly evening of musical theatre. The event brings West End stars to South-east London so that people can enjoy the talent of the West End without the hefty price tag. With the next one due in February 2018, it can be expected to be another sell-out show.

The Alma

Crystal Palace

# The Alma
# REFRIED BLACK BEAN TACOS, TOMATILLO SALSA, AVOCADO, CORN

We use 6-inch corn tortillas from The Cool Chilli Company.

Preparation time: 40 minutes | Cooking time: 30 minutes | Serves 3-4

## Ingredients

**For the tomatillo salsa:**

500g fresh tomatillos

½ bunch coriander

2 limes, juiced

2 green jalapeños

3 garlic cloves

**For the pico de gallo:**

4 ripe tomatoes, deseeded and chopped

1 red onion, finely diced

1 Scotch Bonnet chilli, finely diced

½ bunch coriander, chopped

2 limes, juiced

**For the avocado purée:**

2 ripe avocados

2 limes, juiced

**For the refried black beans:**

1 onion

2 garlic cloves

2 jalapeño chillies, chopped

1 tbsp chipotle, chopped

1 tbsp cumin

1 tsp chilli powder

400g tin of black beans, drained

½ bunch of coriander, chopped

**For the pickled red onions:**

2 red onions, halved and thinly sliced

2 cinnamon sticks

6 whole cloves

Pinch of crushed red pepper flakes

240ml apple cider vinegar

120ml freshly squeezed lime juice

50-100g sugar

1 tbsp Maldon sea salt

**To serve:**

6-inch corn tortillas

Chargrilled corn on the cob, tossed in olive oil, smoked paprika and salt

## Method

**For the tomatillo salsa**

Lightly grill the tomatillos and allow to cool. Put all the ingredients into a blender and blend until smooth. Add salt to taste.

**For the pico de gallo**

Add all the ingredients to a bowl and mix.

**For the avocado purée**

Add all the ingredients to a bowl and mix.

**For the refried black beans**

Fry the onion, garlic and chillies for a few minutes on a low heat. Now add the spices and cook for a few minutes to release the flavours. Add the beans and a cup of water, and simmer on a low-medium heat for 15-20 minutes, stirring frequently. Add the coriander and blend using a whisk. Season with salt to taste.

**For the pickled red onions**

Add the sliced onions to a medium bowl. Pour enough boiling water over so that they are covered. Count to 10, then drain. Add the onions to glass jars (or a glass container with a lid). Toast the cinnamon, cloves and the red pepper flakes in a small saucepan over medium heat until fragrant, for 3-5 minutes. Whisk in the vinegar, lime juice, 50g of the sugar and the salt. Bring to a simmer and cook until the sugar and salt have dissolved, 1-2 minutes. Taste for sweetness, then add more sugar as needed. Pour the brine over the onions. Allow to stand at room temperature until cooled, then cover and refrigerate for up to 2 weeks

**To serve**

Serve in 6-inch corn tortillas with chargrilled corn on the cob tossed in olive oil, smoked paprika and salt.

# *Winning hearts*

# AND MINDS

The Inkspot Brewery, a Streatham-based microbrewery is snuggled within the beautiful Rookery Gardens at the heart of Streatham Common.

## The Inkspot Brewery

The brainchild of the duo behind Art & Craft beer stores, The Inkspot Brewery has come a long way since its inception in 2012 by Tom – a British army officer and beer connoisseur – and Bradley – a restaurateur and urban art collector. Whilst at Bradley's bar/restaurant in Streatham, Tom offered to brew a house beer, 'St Reatham'. It proved so popular with the locals, they decided to formalise their partnership, embark on new careers and formed The Inkspot Brewery.

The brewery name is derived from the Inkspot Strategy, which aims to win the hearts and minds of locals (in this case through beer) and, in doing so, expand an area of influence. Each bar, restaurant or store who stock the beer is designated an Inkspot and becomes part of a growing community.

Set in Edwardian gardens, which are open to the public, the brewery's location lends itself perfectly to sustainable practices and engagement with the local population. The boys plan to use the garden's hops and botanicals in their beer, waste water will be redirected to irrigate the gardens and waste hops will generate heat for the greenhouses. Perhaps the most unique element, however, is a project to access a 17th-century natural spring directly beneath the brewery, which they aim to brew with.

## Art & craft

Excited by the emergence of craft beers in the UK and the success of their first beer in Streatham, the Inkspot boys founded 'Art & Craft SW16', a store stocking hundreds of craft beers, wines, ciders, small batch liquors with urban art on the walls.

With a background in graphic design, Bradley is passionate about how the art world ties in with the burgeoning industry of craft beers – from the craftsmanship of the brew to the beautiful designs on the labels of the bottles and cans they make and sell. Local artists are encouraged to display their work on the walls alongside more established artists, creating a dynamic, rotating range of contemporary art.

Art & Craft SW16 was followed just under a year later by Art & Craft SE27 in West Norwood. So, what is next? A further store in Streatham and an art gallery and bar in Croydon... watch this space.

# The Inkspot Brewery
# SMOKED GOOSE LEG WITH SMOKED TOMATO BEANS

This recipe is from our friends at Brisket and Barrel. Although you need only one bottle of beer to make the recipe, we suggest buying four so you have some to enjoy during the long curing and slow cooking times!

Preparation time: 1 hour, plus 8 hours curing | Cooking time: 6 hours | Serves 4

## Ingredients

**For the goose legs:**

4 goose legs

200g Maldon sea salt

2 twists freshly ground black pepper

1kg goose fat

Cherry/apple wood, for smoking

**For the beans:**

8 ripe plum tomatoes, cut in half

100g dried butter beans, soaked

100g dried cannellini beans, soaked

100g dried chickpeas, soaked

100g dried kidney beans, soaked

2 tbsp goose fat

1 white onion, chopped

2 tbsp tomato paste

3 star anise

4 garlic cloves, crushed

4 bottles of Inkspot Brewery St Reatham Beer (1 for cooking, 3 for drinking!)

Salt and pepper

Herbes de Provence

## Method

**For the goose legs**

Cover the legs lightly with the sea salt and freshly ground black pepper, and refrigerate for 8 hours. Have the first beer. This, in essence, is a light cure, and you'll see that the salt becomes damp as water is absorbed from the goose flesh.

When the 8 hours are up, dab the skin dry using a kitchen towel. Place the goose legs and the fat in an oven tray and smoke at 140°c for 3 hours with cherry/apple wood.

**For the beans**

Put the tomatoes in a tray and add a pinch of salt, pepper and herbes de Provence. Smoke them for half an hour at 110°c. Have the second beer.

Drain the beans and chickpeas then place them in a pan of water. Bring to the boil, then strain and rinse. In a cast-iron pot, heat up a couple of tablespoons of goose fat, then fry the onion. Add the smoked tomato, garlic, a pinch of herbes de Provence, the tomato paste, star anise and, finally, the beans. Cover the mix with 1 bottle of beer. If you need more liquid, add water, simmer for 2 hours. Now it's time to drink the last beer!

After 2 hours, the beans should be soft. Place the goose legs on top. Transfer the pot to the oven at 160°c for 30 minutes. Pop down to Art & Craft to get more beer. Enjoy!

# Art & Craft
# ST JOHNS' BRISKET SANDWICH

This recipe is from our friends at Brisket and Barrel. We would encourage you to make your own mayo and barbecue sauce, if you have the time! If you don't, there is no shame in using good-quality ready-made ones!

Preparation time: 15 minutes | Serves 4

## Ingredients

4 good-quality burger buns (at Brisket and Barrel, we use a croissant-dough bun!)

50ml BBQ sauce

50ml mayonnaise

1 tsp piment d'espelette (red pepper powder)

1 baby gem lettuce

1 beef tomato

400g smoked brisket (we smoke ours at Brisket and Barrel)

4 slices smoked applewood cheddar

2 pickled gherkins

1 bottle of Inkspot Brewery St Reatham Beer, to serve

## Method

Cut the bun in half and toast it for 10 seconds to soften and warm it up.

Mix the BBQ sauce and mayo together, and add as much of the piment d'espelette as your palate can handle.

To build your burger, we recommend starting from the bottom of the bun… add a teaspoon of BBQ mayo, followed by a couple of leaves of baby gem and a generous slice of tomato.

Add the brisket and top it with the cheese. You can melt the cheese with a cook's blow torch, if you have one. Top the cheese with four slices of gherkin, followed by some more BBQ mayo. Add the top of the bun.

Finally, open the beer and enjoy!

### How we smoke our brisket

At Brisket and Barrel, we trim the brisket and coat it with our special rub, then let the brisket rest for 1 hour at room temperature.

We prepare the barbecue for smoking and set the temperature to 115°c.

When the smoker is ready, we place the brisket in it, fat-side up, with the point facing toward the fire. We smoke the brisket for 10-12 hours until the internal temperature reaches 84-86°c. When it's tender it's cooked!

Once we have taken the brisket out of the smoker, we wrap it in foil for 2 hours.

# First-class
# FOOD HALL

Bell & Sons Butchers of Bermondsey is not just a place to buy top-quality meat, it's also where you can be shown how to prepare, cook and serve it.

The description 'food hall' is far more apt for Bell & Sons Butchers, which, along with an impressive meat counter contains a mouth-watering deli stocked with pies, cheeses and freshly baked bread.

Founder Simon Bell, his son Thomas, daughter Hannah and butchery manager Manuel Baptista pride themselves on the family-run ethos – they are always on hand to offer expert advice, dedicated to making sure customers feel relaxed and able to ask questions.

Ask them about the interesting provenance of the meat; prestigious free-range pork comes from Plantation Pigs, pioneers of the first completely free-range system of rearing pigs in the UK. Equally innovative are the free-range herb-fed chickens from the rolling hills of Yorkshire, where the birds forage on ten varieties of fresh herbs daily. They also supply fine turkeys to Bell & Sons, along with another award-winning family-owned poultry farm John Howe from Kent.

Simon says: "Our ethos is that the ethical methods of the way our meat is farmed is of paramount importance. We believe this is vital to the taste, as much as maintaining high standards of animal welfare. I take great care in selecting our suppliers. Our customers tell us this contrasts to supermarkets' bland untraceable products." This is exemplified by Surrey Farm, who supply Bell & Sons with premium grass-fed beef, matured for 21 days, making it natural and tender.

Many customers travel from far away to buy the succulent sausages, which are prepared daily on site. Favourites include Toulouse, Italian, and honey and mustard, which are all hand-made using natural skins. Another favourite is the freshly cooked sausage rolls – all hand-made at Bell & Sons.

Bell & Sons take great pride in their home-cooked beef, turkey and hams on the shop's lively deli counter. Trademark delights include pies, which you can take away and place straight in the oven. Produced by family-run Kentish Mayde, these include chicken, Brie and cranberry, steak and Stilton, steak and kidney, and steak and ale. But there is more to the deli than meat – you will also find a variety of cheeses including Manchego, Cornish Yarg and Comté in the chilled display cabinets.

Despite having opened only four years ago in 2013 (although Simon has been trading in wholesale meat for many years prior to that), Bell & Sons is already firmly on the gastronomic map in Bermondsey and Rotherhithe, not only for home cooks, but with the area's leading restaurants and gastro pubs who love the quality on offer.

# Bell & Sons
# MEDITERRANEAN
# ROLLED PORCHETTA

Succulent slow-roasted pork belly stuffed with fennel seeds and garlic, finished with a deliciously crisp crackling.

Preparation time: 10-15 minutes | Cooking time: 2-2½ hours | Serves 6-8

## Ingredients

2kg Bell & Sons free-range pork belly

50g fresh fennel seeds

4 sprigs of fresh rosemary

1 whole garlic bulb, chopped

Dash of olive oil

Rock salt and black pepper

## Method

Preheat the oven to 210°c. Butterfly the boneless pork belly.

With the skin facing down, season the pork with salt and pepper to taste, followed by the fennel seeds, most of the rosemary, chopped garlic and a dash of oil to finish.

Roll the pork belly into a tight log, and score the skin with a sharp knife. Place a sprig of rosemary on top and tie with string into the perfect roasting joint.

Before placing into the oven, rub oil and salt into the skin for that crisp crackling. Reduce the temperature to 160°c and slow roast for 2-2½ hours.

Remove from the oven and rest for 5-10 minutes, before enjoying with friends and family.

Best served with potatoes, Bramley apple sauce and a glass of red wine.

# *Sweet* TREATS!

A one-stop shop for the good stuff in life, Brett and Bailey are making waves in South London with their approach to cakes and bakes...

The food revolution has long been gathering pace in Britain. Once the laughing stock of the world, we now punch well above our weight in the global village. No meal, however, is complete without that wonderful bit at the end where you say 'I shouldn't, but ...oh, go on then.'

This is the area in which Joe Brett and Matt Bailey excel. Like all good things, it started with passion – the pair are self-taught – and the encouragement of wowed friends inspired them to launch under their own banner and offer their wares for sale. They haven't looked back.

The duo launched Brett and Bailey in December 2012, selling handmade Christmas puddings, panettone and stollen swirls to an appreciative crowd at a pop-up winter market. This first taste of the sweet life got them hooked, and they've since gathered a stellar reputation for all things baked, sweet, sticky, and delicious, with a stall every Saturday at the award-winning Crystal Palace Food Market.

The ethos is simple: drawing on a carefully developed series of master recipes and variations, they make the best cakes, bakes, pies, buns and cookies, using only the best organic flour, eggs and dairy. Oh, and everything is still handmade with love in their small home kitchen.

They place a huge emphasis on seasonality, and their menu changes to reflect the very best of what's available – with some ingredients grown more or less on their doorstep. No wonder that their stall draws loyal regulars, eager to see what the boys have come up with each week.

If it's said that the first bite is with the eye, well, Brett and Bailey's cakes look like they should be framed rather than eaten. However, the proof of the pudding is always in the eating, and the pair were awarded a well-deserved Gold Star in the 2016 Great Taste Awards.

Not only can they be found at an increasing number of South London food markets, but the duo also creates cakes to order, guaranteeing a cake that you'll remember forever, whatever the occasion: a centrepiece at a wedding reception, perhaps, or a luxurious monument to a landmark birthday, or just something to mark an occasion as truly special. Whichever road you take to get there, though, one thing is clear: a visit to Brett and Bailey should be on the cards as soon as possible. This really is the good stuff, beautifully done!

# Brett & Bailey
# CARDAMOM KNOTS

Nordic but nice, this recipe offers a perfect rainy day baking project that
guarantees two great results: a cosy, cardamom-scented kitchen
and a surfeit of sweet, soft, Scandinavian buns.

Preparation time: 3 hours | Cooking time: 20 minutes | Makes 16 knots

## Ingredients

**For the dough:**

725g strong bread flour

300ml whole milk (room temperature)

2 egg yolks

50g fresh yeast (halve the amount if using dried)

½ tsp sea salt

1 tsp ground cardamom (we grind our own for the best flavour)

150g caster sugar

150g unsalted butter (room temperature)

**For the filling:**

3 tsp cinnamon

1 tsp ground cardamom

200g unsalted butter (room temperature)

100g light brown sugar

**To finish:**

1 egg, beaten with a pinch of salt

200g golden syrup

75g water

Ground cardamom

Pearl or caster sugar

## Method

Heat your oven to 170°c (fan). You won't be needing it for a couple of hours, but it'll warm up your kitchen and help give your dough a good rise. Then, in a large bowl, beat together the egg yolks, milk and yeast until the yeast has dissolved. Once you've done this, add the sugar, butter, cardamom, flour and salt and mix it all together before turning it out onto your counter and kneading until you have a dough that's stretchy, springy and silky smooth. Resist adding extra flour – it'll make the end result tough. Shape your dough into a ball, then let it under a strip of cling film and a tea towel in a large, lightly-greased bowl. After an hour or so it will have doubled in size, at least, and be ready for the next step.

While the dough proves, beat together the filling ingredients until you have a pale and creamy mixture. Then, line two large baking sheets – the biggest that will fit in your oven – with greaseproof paper.

Once the dough has risen, dust your counter with a little flour, and roll the dough out into a large rectangle around 5mm thick. Spread your filling over it – right to the edges – and then fold the dough in half as though you're closing a book. Slice it into 16 equally-sized strips of dough – try dividing it in half, then into quarters and so on – a pizza wheel really helps.

Take a strip of dough and, holding one end on the counter, gently stretch it out so it becomes long and thin. Still holding one end down, twist the dough by rolling the other end away from you with the palm of your free hand. Get as many twists in as you can, before rolling it around your finger a couple of times and tucking the end through the middle to make your knot. Place on your prepared baking sheet and repeat until you have your full batch of knots. Cover each tray with a lightly-greased strip of cling film and a tea towel, and then leave them to rise for another hour.

Beat the egg and salt together, then lightly brush each bun. Bake for 18-20 minutes, or until a deep golden brown. While they're baking, heat the water and golden syrup together and whisk until combined and runny. Once the buns are baked, brush them liberally with syrup, before sprinkling them with more ground cardamom and pearl sugar.

Try and leave them to cool, but be warned… it's impossible not to have a warm one!

# Brett & Bailey
# STRAWBERRY FIZZ CAKE

This decadent layer cake is a perfect way to make a summer occasion truly special. We use our favourite prosecco, but you could break the bank and go for Champagne instead. Either way, wait until strawberries are at their very best.

Preparation time: 2 hours | Cooking time: 1 hour | Serves 12-15

## Ingredients

285g plain flour

285g unsalted butter (room temperature)

285g golden caster sugar

2½ tsps baking powder

5 large eggs

80ml prosecco (room temperature)

½ tsp salt

**For the prosecco buttercream:**

4 large egg whites

½ tsp salt

300g granulated sugar

45g water

450g unsalted butter (room temperature)

200ml prosecco (room temperature)

**To finish:**

500g strawberries

Strawberry jam

Red food colour gel

Edible glitter

1 tsp vodka

## Method

Heat the oven to 160°c (fan). Grease a 9" round springform cake tin, line the bottom with parchment, and dust the sides with flour.

To make the sponge, beat together the butter and sugar until light and creamy.

Whisk together the flour, baking powder and salt, then add a tablespoonful to the butter mixture and thoroughly fold in – this will give your sponge a tender crumb. Beat in the eggs one at a time until well combined, before folding in the rest of the flour. Then stream in the prosecco – make sure it doesn't have a foamy head, as this will introduce too much air into your mixture and make your cake sink. Smooth into your prepared cake tin with a spatula, and bake for around an hour. When ready, the middle of the sponge will spring back if lightly pushed. Let it cool for 15 minutes before removing from the tin and setting aside to cool completely.

To make the prosecco buttercream, place the egg whites in a large clean bowl with the salt and two tablespoons of the granulated sugar. Whisk until frothy. Stir together the remaining sugar and water in a saucepan, and heat until it reaches 115°c on a sugar thermometer. While whisking the egg whites at high speed – and we recommend a stand mixer for this – stream the melted sugar into them, and continue to whisk for around 10 minutes or until you have a thick, fluffy, glossy meringue. Set aside to cool.

Once your meringue has cooled, whisk in the room temperature butter – around 50g at a time – until it's all mixed in and you have a rich, smooth, fluffy buttercream. While continuing to whisk at low speed, add the prosecco a little at a time until thoroughly combined.

### To finish

Slice the sponge into three layers of equal depth. Spread the bottom layer with jam and fistfuls of chopped strawberries, then smooth over a layer of buttercream. Add the middle layer and repeat, before placing the final layer on top and covering the reassembled cake with most of the remaining buttercream – a palette knife or a dough scraper will help you get smooth, neat sides. Put your cake in the fridge for 15 minutes, or until the buttercream is firm.

Mix a tablespoon of buttercream with a teaspoon of jam and a drop or two of red colouring. Dab this onto the cake, and spread it around with your palette knife to give a smeared effect. Return to the fridge until set.

Mix edible glitter with a splash of vodka until just slightly runny, then paint onto the cake as you wish. Finish with the remaining strawberries and serve.

# *All round* GOOD EGGS

With Brown & Green's cafés popping up just a few miles from each other over the past few years, twin sisters Laura and Jess Tilli appear to be taking over South London...

In a crowded, competitive marketplace to open and run one successful café is a signal achievement. If one becomes five, well, then you're definitely doing something right! The success of Brown & Green around the Crystal Palace and Sydenham areas can be put down to many things. For a start, Laura and Jess are local girls, and are incredibly proud to be part of and serving what they describe as their 'wonderful local community.'

This passion comes through in their approach. Brown & Green are a cluster of what the sisters call 'Brunch Kitchens' as much as they are cafés. Each serves what might best be called 'the classics', but while with so many apparently easy things its equally easy to get them wrong, with Brown and Green the devil is in the detail – and they get them spectacularly right. Take the Aussie Eggs, for example, which takes the brunch standard of scrambled eggs and combines them with smashed avocado on sourdough toast before dishing them up with vegemite, rocket, and sweet chilli sauce. Or The Bubbly which serves up a classic Full English with a glass of prosecco to really start your day off fizzingly.

It isn't all twist, with staples like Bacon Butties, homemade soups and salads all benefiting from an approach that sources the best produce. All of the girls' cafes are hugely kid friendly so that Mums, Dads, and children can all get together and eat some of the good stuff on the menu while taking some much needed rest and recuperation. Supper Clubs have also taken off at the Triangle, bringing together exciting new guest chefs and hungry locals to explore new flavours and approaches to food. It isn't only a haven for those dropping by either. Brown and Green are also building a stellar reputation as a great place to book out for your party.

Going from strength to strength, with Brown & Green it might well be a case of today, South London; tomorrow, the world!

# Brown and Green
# AUSSIE EGGS

Laura and Jess liven up a standard Sunday scramble with a delicious Tilli twist on an all-time favourite breakfast!

Preparation time: 5 minutes | Cooking time: 10 minutes | Serves 2

## Ingredients

6 free-range eggs

4 slices of your favourite bread (we love rye, but our husbands prefer this on a big hunk of crusty baguette!)

1 tsp butter, plus extra for spreading

Vegemite (if you REALLY can't find it you can use Marmite!)

1-2 ripe avocados

2 handfuls rocket

Sweet chilli sauce

Pinch of salt

Pinch of pepper

## Method

Squash the avocados in a bowl with a fork and season to taste.

Whisk the eggs together in a bowl with a pinch of salt and pepper before melting a teaspoon of butter in a nonstick pan over a low heat.

Add the eggs to the pan and stir gently.

While this is cooking, toast the bread. Butter it whilst hot, and slather on plenty of Vegemite and the squashed avocado.

When the eggs are softly cooked, spoon them over the avocado on toast and top with a handful of rocket. Drizzle with the sweet chilli sauce. Done!

Serve immediately with a steaming hot cuppa. Sit back and enjoy!

# *Perfect* PLATTERS

At the heart of Bermondsey Street's thriving foodie district, B Street Deli is known as one of the city's favourite spots to enjoy cheeses, charcuterie, sandwiches, coffee and fine wines.

B Street Deli is a vibrant deli that showcases the very best of traditional artisan foods in a trend-setting, contemporary atmosphere, making it perfectly suited to its home at the heart of historic Bermondsey – an area that today buzzes as one of the capital's gastronomic hotspots.

With the London Bridge Quarter and the Shard, Borough Market and Maltby St Market all close by, it is easy to see why this destination has become a firm favourite for Londoners in the know. And at the heart of it lies B Street Deli, known as the home of the best sandwiches, platters and coffee in Bermondsey.

The deli counter comprises a mouth-watering collection of British and European offerings, all of which have been selected for their quality and taste by the expert 'food hunters' at B Street Deli. From artisan cheeses and fine charcuterie to fresh olives and antipasti, the deli counter is a food-lover's paradise that takes your taste buds on a journey across Europe.

Alongside the traditional deli service, there is a long bar where customers can take a seat and enjoy breakfast, lunch and evening menus, accompanied by fine wine by the glass or

bottle. Special evening platters feature the best products from behind the deli counter. Being both a classic deli and a relaxed wine bar, B Street Deli is a foodie destination that simply lets the food and drink take centre stage.

The helpful staff are knowledgeable about their products, and they love to help diners and shoppers find the perfect taste. They also make up exotic deli sandwiches, fresh soups, savoury pastries, and platters of cheese, charcuterie, seafood and antipasti. B Street Deli also caters for both private and corporate breakfasts, luncheons and dinners with sumptuous platters, whether it's a small meeting or a large drinks party.

With carefully selected wines from small and artisan producers served alongside fine teas and speciality coffees, there is always the ideal drink to match the chosen food. So, whether it is afternoon tea with cakes and pastries or a deli platter with a glass of wine, B Street Deli is a place where traditional appreciation of artisan foods is celebrated in a warm, welcoming and convivial atmosphere.

# B Street Deli
# MIXED CHEESE AND CHARCUTERIE BOARD

Adding some mixed antipasti to this selection of cheese and charcuterie from B Street Deli adds an extra element of texture.

Preparation time: 15 minutes | Serves 4

## Ingredients

1 tbsp extra-virgin olive oil

Balsamic vinegar, to taste

50g mixed leaves and rocket

250g prosciutto, Serrano ham or coppa parma, sliced paper-thin

1-2 saucisson sec or salami, whole or thinly sliced

100g sheep's milk cheese, cut into wedges

100g aged goat's milk cheese, cut into wedges

100g cow's milk cheese, cut into wedges

Mixed antipasti, to garnish

Sea salt and freshly ground pepper

## Method

In a large bowl, using a fork, mix together the olive oil, vinegar and ¼ teaspoon salt. Season to taste with pepper. Add the mixed leaves and toss lightly to coat. Arrange the dressed greens on one side of a serving platter.

Slice the prosciutto, Serrano ham or coppa parma into paper-thin slices. Thinly slice the saucisson sec or salami, or leave it whole. Cut the sheep's, goat's and cow's milk cheeses into wedges.

Arrange the meats and cheeses around the salad on the platter, and add the antipasti, building the height as you radiate out. Serve immediately.

# *Simple* PLEASURES

A new destination on the beer map of South London, microbrewery Canopy Beer Co is bringing great beer to the locals of Herne Hill from its hidden location.

Hidden under the railway arches in Herne Hill, a stone's throw from Brockwell Park, you will find Canopy Beer Co; a brewery and tap room that has been brewing small batch beers since 2014. The emphasis is on drinkable, accessible beers made with minimal intervention – no filtration, no finings and no pasteurisation. The beers are big, juicy and jammed full of flavour.

Herne Hill locals Matthew and Estelle Theobalds decided that SE24 deserved its own neighbourhood brewery and so Canopy Beer Co was born. Local enthusiasm and support has been key to the growth of both the brewery and the on-site tap room since it was established, and the beer is now widely available throughout London and beyond.

Seasonality is the cornerstone of the brewery ethos – early autumn brings the annual Green Hop beer, brewed using hops grown in Brixton and Herne Hill gardens and allotments; winter heralds the arrival of the coveted Imperial Stout, with a different version created each year – look out for the barrel-aged versions too. Spring and summer mark the arrival of seasonal pale ales – light, juicy and perfect for a picnic in the park.

If you venture down to visit the brewery itself, then in the midst of a plethora of brewing equipment, a small bar welcomes you – with 10 keg lines and an occasional cask, there's plenty of choice from the Canopy Beer Co range, and usually a local or exotic guest beer on tap too. Tasting flights, local snacks and a cosy atmosphere make this friendly tap room a must for locals and visitors alike. All are amazed that all brewing, bottling, kegging and canning takes place on-site in the compact brewery.

Welcoming cyclists, parents, singles, couples and groups, young and old alike, the tap room defies categorisation. Everyone is welcome and everyone comes – friendships are forged over a beer. The tap room offers more than just a drink though, hosting film festivals and music nights, pop-up food events, hop festivals, tasting events and yard parties. One thing is for sure: nothing – apart from the excellent beer – stays the same for long at Canopy Beer Co.

Drink. Enjoy.

LOVE LONDON
AWARDS 2016
WINNER
SUPPORTED BY
MAYOR OF LONDON

# CANOPY BEER CO

LAST CHANCE!

CANOPY
BEER CO
BROCKWELL IPA
BREWED IN HERNE HILL

CANOPY
BEER CO
CHAMPION KÖLSCH
BREWED IN HERNE HILL

CANOPY
BEER CO
SUNRAY PALE ALE
BREWED IN HERNE HILL

CANOPY
BEER CO
FULL MOON PORTER
BREWED IN HERNE HILL

# Canopy Beer Co.
# FULL MOON PORTER CHOCOLATE CAKE

To put beer in a cake sounds odd – but it adds delicious moisture. If you're going to make a chocolate cake, make it with a porter! This recipe was inspired by Nigella Lawson's Chocolate Guinness Cake, and follows her method. However, rather than Guinness, we use our Full Moon Porter, which gives the cake an amazing richness. Sour cream icing gives a lovely sharp contrast to the deep dense sponge.

Preparation time: 30 minutes | Cooking time: 1 hour | Serves 12

## Ingredients

### For the cake:

250ml Full Moon Porter

250g unsalted butter

90g cocoa powder

200g soft light brown sugar

200g caster sugar

140ml sour cream

2 large eggs

1 tbsp vanilla extract

275g plain four

2½ tsp bicarbonate of soda

### For the icing:

100g sour cream

100g cream cheese

50g butter

1 tsp vanilla extract

250g icing sugar

## Method

### For the cake

Preheat the oven to 180°c/350°f/gas mark 4. Grease and line a 23cm spring-form cake tin.

Heat the Full Moon Porter and butter in a saucepan until the butter has melted. Add the cocoa powder, light brown sugar and caster sugar, and whisk everything together.

Put the sour cream and the eggs in a bowl, and beat them together. Add them to the pan with the vanilla and stir well. Add the flour and bicarbonate of soda, and whisk in.

Pour the batter into the cake tin and bake for 45 minutes to 1 hour. Leave to cool completely in the tin on a cooling rack. Once cooled, turn it out of the tin and place on a serving plate.

### For the icing

Mix together the sour cream, cream cheese, butter and vanilla. Sift in the icing sugar and carefully beat everything together until smooth. Split the cake into two halves and sandwich with the icing. Spread the remaining icing on top of the cake.

# *Best of* BRITISH

A quality family-run butchers, Chadwicks has been providing organic and rare-breed lamb, beef and pork to Balham since 1999.

When it comes to good-quality traditional British meat, there is not much that Balham's favourite butchers, Chadwicks, don't know. They have been a famous fixture of the community since 1999 when the business was started by butcher Gary Chadwick and his wife Jennie.

A trained butcher with 35 years in the meat industry, Gary is also bilingual, had gained a BA (hons) degree and spent years working in the corporate world, developing his branding, store layout, business analysis and customer communication skills. Gary gradually got more and more disillusioned with the corporate world, while also getting increasingly fed up with not being able to buy decent meat in his local area. Eventually he took the plunge to solve both of these problems – and in 1999 he and Jennie opened Chadwicks in Balham.

They have come a long way from the first day when they took just £68 – today the business turns over more than £1 million a year. Gary has achieved this by focusing on the quality of his meat. He works with local farmers to get the best beef, pork and lamb, which have been farmed in traditional ways. They also stock a range of branded preserves, mustards and stocks amongst many other accompaniments.

Gary is a champion of British butchers. As well as being Chairman of the Q Guild of Butchers, he has also spent many an hour working with the government to improve the perception of the butchery business and help small businesses grow. He worked closely with the then Secretary of State for Business, Innovation and Skills, Vince Cable, and Lord Curry to extend his own experiences of running a small butchery business into practical changes of policy.

After an expansion in 2009, Chadwicks were always being asked by customers when they would open another store. Finally, in 2015, Gary and Jennie opened a second shop in Tooting Broadway, providing more access to quality meat to more of South London.

When he isn't sitting around a table with MPs or standing behind the counter in his shop, football fan Gary has become known for his multiple appearances on TV – most notably when he explained the concept of relegation using a host of butchery metaphors, as the face of the Premier League in the USA and China! For Chadwicks, however, there is no talk of relegation… their journey in the top flight just keeps going from strength to strength.

# Chadwicks
# THE HOBBIT PIE

In 2001 Chadwick's butchers was commissioned to make 500 puff pastry pies for the premier party of the blockbuster film The Lord of the Rings in Leicester square. Little did we know that a BBC journalist would use the pies as a backdrop and report, "all the stars are eating Hobbit pies". Since that day, Chadwick's butchers has been known as the home of the Hobbit pie.

Preparation time: 20 minutes, plus cooling | Cooking time: 2½-3 hours | Serves 4-6

## Ingredients

1 large onion, finely diced

1½kg beef skirt, diced into 2½cm squares

1-2 tbsp plain flour

500ml beef stock

500ml red wine

2 tbsp flour, for rolling out the pastry

1 tbsp olive oil

200-300g shortcrust pastry

400-500g puff pastry

Salt and pepper

Oil, for cooking

Butter, for greasing

Beaten egg, for brushing

## Method

Heat a little oil in a wok until hot, then add the onion. After 1 minute, add the diced meat and turn it until it is brown. Reduce heat, add the flour and turn the meat again, making sure all the meat is covered in the flour.

Add the stock and the wine along with a pinch each of salt and pepper to a pressure cooker or pan. Put over a medium heat, add the meat and cover with a lid. If cooking in a pressure cooker, wait until the top is steaming then reduce to a low heat and cook for a further 20 minutes. If using a lidded pan, simmer on a low heat for 1½-2 hours.

Once cooked, stir well and make sure the stock is reduced and thickened, then cool the meat in the fridge (for better results cook the meat the day before).

Preheat the oven to 170-180°c. Line a large pie dish with a smother of butter or olive oil. Take the shortcrust pastry and roll it out until it's not too thick, around 5mm, and line the dish. Trim the excess pastry, ensuring you have a slight overhang over the lip of the pie dish.

Add the meat and stock into the dish; you will know if your stock is thick enough as it will have congealed on cooling. Use the egg wash to brush around the top of the pastry.

Roll out the puff pastry to twice the thickness of the shortcrust pastry, egg wash around the outside pastry which will make contact with the shortcrust pastry and place over the top of the dish. Use a knife, fork or your fingers to crimp the pastry. Use a knife to remove any excess pastry. Make two slits in the middle of the pie using a knife, so that any steam can escape. Wash with the beaten egg.

For best cooking results place a dish of water in the bottom of the oven (this stops the pastry from drying out) and cook the pie for 40-45 minutes until golden brown.

# *Authentic and* AROMATIC

London Bridge is home to one of London's finest Asian restaurants, Champor-Champor – a unique Thai-Malay dining experience with a focus on flavours, presentation and atmosphere.

Tucked away behind London Bridge station, at the back of Guy's Hospital, Champor-Champor is a hidden culinary gem that takes the diner from the centre of London to the heart of Thailand. Walls adorned with tribal artefacts and Buddha statues surround the restaurant to create an interesting ambience, which is helped by the warmth of deep reds, soft lighting and flickering candles.

It was taken over by Bee, Som and Narong in 2012. They retained some connection to the venue's previous guise as a Malaysian fusion restaurant, for example keeping its name, Champor-Champor, which translates from Malay as 'mix and match'. However, they also had lots of new ideas for the new venture, mainly to put authentic Thai cuisine at its heart.

Being from Thailand herself, Bee was keen to bring the aromas, spices and flavours of traditional Thai cuisine to the restaurant. For Bee, their success is down to the consistency of the cooking by chefs Narong and Kittipop. The quality, quantity and taste is always reliable.

The menu at Champor-Champor fuses some European ingredients with typical Thai and Malay spice mixes, for example the lamb shank braised in blue Sumatra coffee, red wine and dried red chilli. The green curry is one of the most popular dishes; either with king prawns or grilled chicken thighs. The classic Malaysian dish beef rendang is also one of her bestsellers; a dish Bee kept on the menu from the restaurant's previous owners.

Champor-Champor has many vegan and vegetarian regulars, who come back time and time again to taste its many meat- and dairy-free options. Think green papaya, crispy tofu, pomegranate somtam and roasted cashew nuts to start, followed by baked fresh shitake, potato edamame dumpling, Szechuan peppercorn sauce and toasted pine nuts.

An adventurous wine list complements the bold flavours of the food, but there are also many beers, spirits, liqueurs, teas, coffees, herbal infusions and soft drinks available too.

For an escape from the hustle and bustle of central London, there is nowhere quite like Champor-Champor. More than just a restaurant, this is a unique dining experience that captivates its diners as soon as soon as they walk inside.

# Champor-Champor
# KING RIVER PRAWNS, YELLOW TURMERIC CURRY, EGG, CREAM, CELERY

This super-quick dish is whipped up in about 5 minutes in the restaurant, and must be served straight away. It also boasts the many health benefits of turmeric.

Preparation time: 10 minutes | Cooking time: 10 minutes | Serves 1

## Ingredients

**For the curry:**

4 tbsp oil, for cooking

2 garlic cloves, finely chopped

5 slices mixed colour peppers

5 slices celery

3 tbsp Chinese white wine

2 tbsp oyster sauce

½ tsp turmeric powder

2 tsp sugar

4 tbsp Carnation milk

½ egg

**For the prawns:**

2 large prawns

Egg, beaten, for coating

Flour, for dusting

Oil, for deep-frying

## Method

### For the curry

Heat the cooking oil in a frying pan or wok and add the chopped garlic. Add the sliced mixed pepper and celery, then add the Chinese white wine. Stir-fry to mix all the ingredients well.

Add the oyster sauce, turmeric powder and sugar, and stir well. Then add the Carnation milk and mix it well again. Turn off the heat. Finally add the egg, and quickly stir it through.

### For the prawns

Heat the oil for deep-frying. Coat the prawns in egg and then the flour, then deep-fry until cooked. Serve the prawns with the curry immediately.

# The GOOD STUFF

This award-winning, sister-run fine chocolatier is building an impressive reputation, expanding what can be done with chocolate, and introducing us to more moments of chocolatey wonderfulness … which can only be a good thing!

Opportunity, they say, is part of a triangle of elements. The other two supporting sides in the equation are luck and preparation. Lucky, then, that Emma Pattenden discovered a passion for Belgian chocolate while working for Eurostar back in the 1990's. Lucky, too, that she had a solid background in Food Technology to help her explore this passion in-depth. Oh, and it's definitely fortuitous that her sister Louise shared her passion and helped bring Chocolates by Eloise to the world.

The name reflects the kindred spirit of the two sisters and their commitment to their shared mission: to take the best approach to producing fine Belgian chocolate while adding in the influences of their London background. The results are chocolate bars, slabs, and pralines made with the highest quality ingredients. The classics that you might expect are all present and correct, but there are some interesting twists that you might not. For example, Chocolate by Eloise's Extra Dark Bar might boast an impressive 72% concentration of cocoa in its make-up, but it's the addition of the richness of Sour Cherries alongside the distinctive bite of Fennel that makes it an intriguing confection – and a hit. It's currently one of Chocolate by Eloise's best-sellers.

Their approach is award-winning. Their Extra Dark Chocolate with Ginger and Lemongrass bar has just won a Great Taste Award for its delicious flavour combination. More than that, their hard work, dedication and amazing chocolate are deservedly reaching wider audiences all the time too. The sisters are mainstays at some of the best farmers' markets and Food Festivals, including South London's vibrant Herne Hill Farmers' Market. Their wonderful work is also carried by some of the staple outlets of South London's burgeoning food scene, including Dugard & Daughters and Bayley & Sage. Everything is handmade too, and done so with the passion and expertise that launched Emma and Louise off on their journey in the first place.

So, if chocolate be the food of love (and everyday life), down at Chocolates by Eloise, well, they're cooking up a symphony!

# Chocolates by Eloise

## CRUNCHY SALTED CARAMEL SHARDS

The clue is in the title as Chocolate by Eloise reference their native London architecture in this mix of contrasting flavours and textures. Easy to make, delicious to eat, go on … be a devil!

Preparation time: 15 minutes | Cooking time: 40 minutes | Serves 4

## Ingredients

### For the shards

200g unsalted butter

250g caster sugar

4g sea salt

400g extra dark chocolate

### Equipment

Hand whisk

Thermometer

Shallow baking tin

Silicone mat/cellophane

## Method

Using a clean, dry heavy-bottomed saucepan, heat the butter, sugar and salt until the ingredients are completely melted. Stir occasionally to ensure even heat distribution and be careful: this mixture will be extremely hot!

Continue to heat the mixture until the colour begins to turn brown. Using a sugar thermometer, check the temperature has reached 146°c.

Turning off the heat, continue to mix by hand with a whisk to make sure that the ingredients emulsify as they cool into a smooth, combined mixture. Then pour immediately into a non-stick baking tray to a depth of around 5mm. Allow this to cool before placing in the refrigerator.

While this is cooling, place 300g of chocolate into a microwaveable bowl and heat on high power for 30 seconds. Stir and repeat at 10 second intervals until the chocolate has melted and reaches 45°c.

Adding the remaining 100g of chocolate, stir continuously until it has melted and the chocolate cools and thickens slightly. This process is called 'tempering' and it is essential to ensure a smooth, shiny finish. To check that has tempered correctly, dip a palette knife into the mixture and leave for a couple of minutes to cool. Check the finish. If it has not yet tempered, continue to stir and cool.

Once the desired finish has been achieved, remove the cooled caramel from the tin by tipping it out and breaking it into shards. Dip each shard in the cooled melted chocolate, making sure that all caramel is covered and then place it onto a silicone or cellophane covered baking sheet and place in the refrigerator until they have set.

Eat, and enjoy. (These also look great bagged up as gifts!)

# *Freshly*
# BAKED

Set within the leafy streets between North Dulwich and Herne Hill, Christopher's bakery and deli is a local gem for lovers of freshly-baked bread, handmade croissants and home-cooked food.

Since it opened in June 2015, Christopher's has been filling the air with the irresistible aroma of baking bread and brewing coffee. From their classic Dulwich sourdough to the vollkornbrot (sunflower rye) and croissants, every loaf and every pastry is made from scratch on the premises, throughout the day.

The bakery belongs to Christopher Garner who, after 25 years working in HR, decided to retrain and do something to satisfy his inner foodie. Thanks to a career that allowed him to travel the world, Christopher had been lucky enough to sample delicious, authentic food and drink from around the globe. Inspired by his experiences, he wanted to bring the very best bread, cheeses and cured meats to his community in South-east London.

His food career started in his home kitchen, where he baked with his daughter, Tiffanni, the namesake of one of Christopher's most popular loaves, the bloomer. Soon, their creations were so in demand, he opened Christopher's. He has grown the business slowly and organically over the last two years – gradually taking on staff members who receive weeks of training before starting their baking journey.

He credits his family for their help in the early days. His brother, Nicholas, designed the front and interior of the building; his sister, Geraldine, was instrumental in spreading the word about its opening; and his wife, Suanne, is often found working in the kitchen as a chef. His initial business partner, Stefan Balachandran, was also vital in setting up the business.

Today, Christopher's isn't just becoming well-known in London; he has French customers taking his croissants and pain au chocolat back to France, as well as German customers who travel from far and wide to buy his authentic rye breads.

Alongside the lovingly made sandwiches and pastries, you'll find great coffee, salads, soups and quiches, as well as take-home deli items. "With everything we make, it all comes down to using top-quality ingredients," explains Christopher, who sources his meat from William Rose in Dulwich, amongst other small suppliers from across the capital.

Their food philosophy is simple; everything they make is something that Christopher himself loves. The menu reflects both his and his wife's tastes. For Christopher, there's nothing better than a fresh baguette and some tasty cheese. For Suanne, it's all about colourful salads. It's a business you have to be passionate about, and for the owner of Christopher's, it's a labour of love.

# Christopher's Bakery
## DULWICH SOURDOUGH

This sourdough is typical of the bread we make at Christopher's. It begins with the creation of an organic dark rye sourdough starter. It may seem a lengthy process, and of course you can make bread much more quickly, but you won't get the same flavour or texture. Alternatively let us do all the hard work and come to Christopher's!

Preparation time: Up to 10 days | Cooking time: 35 minutes | Makes 1 loaf

## Ingredients

**For the sourdough starter:**

350g organic dark rye flour

525g water

**For the bread:**

45g sourdough starter

606g organic untreated white flour

370g water

10g salt

## Method

**For the sourdough starter:**

Day 1: Mix 50g of organic dark rye flour with 75g of water, cover loosely and set aside.

Day 2: Add another 50g of organic dark rye flour and 75 grams of water. Mix, cover loosely and set aside.

Day 3: Discard half of the mixture and add 50g of organic dark rye flour with 75 grams of water. Mix, cover loosely and set aside.

Days 4-10: Repeat Day 3 for the next 5-7 days. Nature will take its course and you will have created your sourdough starter.

**For the bread:**

Day 1: Create a barm, by mixing 45g of your new starter with 95g of organic untreated white flour and 118g of water. Cover loosely and set aside. Remember to refresh (feed) your starter, with the same weight you removed (ratio 3:2, water:flour). Continue to do this while you want to keep it.

Day 2: Combine your barm with 511g of organic untreated white flour, 252g of water and 10g of salt. Knead by hand for about 10 minutes. You can use a mixer with a dough hook if you prefer. In general, it is better to under mix than over mix! Fold the dough three times within the next 90 minutes (letting it rest in between), then shape the dough and place top-side down in a lined banetton. Place the banetton in the fridge overnight.

Day 3: Place a baking stone and narrow container (such as a ramekin or baking tray) that can hold water, into the oven and preheat to 230°c. Once the stone is fully heated, tip the dough out of the banetton, so it is now top-side up, and score the dough as you wish in order to control how the dough blooms. Place on the baking stone and pour about 50g of water into the narrow container to produce steam. Bake for 15 minutes with the narrow steam container in, then open the oven, take the container out, and bake for a further 20 minutes or until the internal temperature of the bread is 91°c. Allow the bread time to cool and enjoy!

Please look up any obscure terms such 'folding dough' or 'lined banetton' on the internet if you haven't come across them before.

# Food from THE HEART

Serving up nourishing, comforting and delicious dishes for the last 15 years, Comfort and Joy is well known at South London's food markets.

Comfort and Joy is owned by artist Andrea Adjei. The business was inspired by and named after her mum, Comfort, a passionate cook who instilled into her daughter a love of freshly cooked food.

Andrea reflects now that she never expected to run her own food business. She graduated with a degree in Fine Arts and an appreciation of all things creative. However, she soon realised that her artistic background was perfectly suited to her lifelong appreciation of good food – Andrea considers colour, texture and design when she is cooking and plating up food.

Comfort and Joy started life as a market stall on Northcross Road in East Dulwich. Andrea devised dishes that took inspiration from all over the globe. For her, it's all about taste. "I cook food I like," she explains, "it's comforting, but not necessarily what we think of as 'comfort food' – I make up to 14 salads a day, bean burgers, oven-baked falafel, veggie Scotch eggs, fish cakes, sausage rolls and so much more."

More often than not, restaurant menus contain a majority of meat and fish dishes with only a small amount of veggie options. Andrea turns this concept on its head and makes vegetarian and vegan food the focus of her cooking, complemented by a choice selection of meat and fish dishes.

Her Thai chickpea curry is a popular choice thanks to being both vegan and gluten-free.

Crystal Palace and Norwood markets were soon added to her busy schedule and Andrea has nothing but appreciation and warmth for her fantastic team who work hard alongside her with honesty and commitment.

Along with the markets and a thriving catering service, Comfort and Joy also has a permanent home in the form of a local café on Church Road, Upper Norwood.

The café opens for a limited time each week – Wednesday to Friday, 12-3pm – and welcomes a host of regulars. A secret gem, people who don't know about the café are unlikely to walk in, but if they do, they are greeted with original art-lined walls (all by Andrea herself), a cosy atmosphere and an ever-changing menu.

For foodies in the know, Comfort and Joy is a feast for all the senses – vibrant, healthy, flavourful and aromatic food, or, to be more precise, this is food made with love.

WRAPS
MADE TO ORDER

# Comfort and Joy
# OVEN-BAKED FALAFELS

To make these tasty falafels, you will need to soak your chickpeas overnight, so make sure you start preparations the day before you plan to serve them.

Preparation time: 20 minutes, plus soaking | Cooking time: 2 hours | Makes 10

## Ingredients

250g dried chickpeas

2 medium-sized sweet potatoes (preferably yellow), peeled and chopped into rough chunks

2 garlic cloves

½ onion, chopped

1 small bunch flat-leaf parsley

1 small bunch coriander

½ tsp ground coriander

½ tsp ground cumin

Salt and pepper

## Method

Soak the chickpeas overnight in cold water. The next day, drain them, rinse and cook until tender. Drain well and leave aside until dry. Once dry, blend them until they are a flour-like consistency.

Preheat the oven to 160°c. Place the potatoes in a baking tray with enough oil to coat. Cover with foil and roast until softened. Leave the oven on ready to cook the falafels.

Blend the potatoes with the garlic, the onion, the parsley and the coriander. Mix with the chickpea flour and season with the spices and salt and pepper to taste.

Shape the falafels in small balls, the size of ping pong balls, and then flatten with your hand. Place on a baking tray lined with baking paper.

Bake the falafels for 20-30 minutes, depending on the strength of your oven.

# *Authentic Argentine* ATMOSPHERE

Bringing the spirit of the Pampas to London's ancient tannery and leather district, Constancia has found its perfect home in Bermondsey.

Since it first opened its doors in May 2009, Sebastian Harguindey's Argentine grill quickly gained a reputation for the quality of its charcoal-grilled steaks, famous empanadas, Iberico pork and exclusively Argentinian wine list, not to mention the attentive service and friendly atmosphere.

The restaurant is owned by Sebastian Harguindey, who moved to London from Argentina and fell in love with the hospitality industry. Little did he know at the time, but the iconic area he chose to open his steak house was very apt – his restaurant's new home was once the leather district of the capital, which not only makes it the perfect place to celebrate beef, but he also discovered that his family used to run tanneries in Spain.

Bringing the beef back to Bermondsey was a labour of love for Sebastian. It was welcomed onto the local food scene with rave reviews thanks to the premium meat from Argentina.

In Argentina, the cows roam the open grasslands freely, which, being remarkably flat, requires little effort, and therefore less hard-working muscle. Grass-fed beef also boasts lower fat content, higher vitamin and mineral content, and more omega-3, as well as being deliciously tender and tasty when cooked on the authentic charcoal parrilla.

Contancia is also known for its homemade empanadas, which became famous when they appeared in Paul Hollywood's Pies & Puds on the BBC. These delicious filled pastries have now become so popular that they have decided to share their recipe in this book, too.

Passionate about food, Sebastian's mouth-watering menu is made up of the finest ingredients available, many from nearby Borough Market, and it aims to showcase the amazing cuisine of his home country. This includes the wine list too, of course, which is made up entirely of Argentinian wines from the renowned Mendoza region, as well as wines from San Juan, Salta and Patagonia.

Many of the desserts are made by Sebastian's aunt, and include gooey homemade chocolate brownie with dulce de leche, as well as a dulce de leche cheesecake – both of which provide a truly decadent ending to an authentic Argentinean meal.

Constancia

# Constancia
# BEEF EMPANADAS

Serve these empanadas either hot or cold, as a snack or starter.
Empanadas can also be filled with ham and cheese, cheese and onion,
spinach and cheese, or many other combinations.

Preparation time: 1 hour, plus 2-3 hours cooling, plus 40 minutes resting |
Cooking time: 45 minutes | Serves 4

## Ingredients

### For the filling:

2 tbsp olive oil

750g onions, finely chopped

250g spring onions, finely chopped

1 red pepper, chopped

500g lean minced beef

75g raisins

1 tsp smoked paprika

Pinch of dry cumin

Pinch of ground red pepper

Pinch of salt

2 hard-boiled eggs, roughly chopped

100g green olives, pitted and roughly
chopped

### For the dough:

Large pinch of salt

125ml water, at room temperature

500g plain flour (0000 preferably)

110g lard

1 egg, plus 1 egg, beaten, to finish

## Method

### For the filling

Heat the oil in a large pan, add the onions, spring onions and red pepper, and fry, stirring continuously, until the onions are soft and translucent. Add the beef and break it down with a wooden spoon. Once the beef and onions have been mixed and cooked for about 2 minutes, add the raisins, paprika, cumin, ground pepper and salt. Once the beef is cooked, and you are satisfied with the seasoning, set the filling with its juices to one side, and let it cool for 2-3 hours. (It is even better if, once cool, you leave it in the fridge overnight).

### For the dough

Dissolve the salt in the water. Cut the lard into 1cm cubes. On a clean work surface, make a crown with the flour and place the lard and the egg in the centre. Add some water and start mixing. Add just enough water and knead to form a soft, silky dough. Place in a bowl, cover and set aside to rest for 40 minutes. Place back onto a floured surface and roll out to a thin sheet, 2mm thick. Cut out 18 discs of pastry using a 12cm cutter.

Preheat the oven to 180°c/350°f/Gas 4.

### To fill the empanadas

Place a tablespoon of the filling on the centre of each pastry circle, add a little hard-boiled egg and olive. Brush the edge with water, fold over and crimp the edges together. Brush with the beaten egg and place on a greased baking sheet. Bake for 20-25 minutes, or until golden-brown.

# A Family AFFAIR

Located in one of Herne Hill's evocative Victorian railway arches, this family-run butchers and larder has carved out a glowing reputation since opening in 2013.

Husband-and-wife team Neil and Rosie Dugard had lived in Herne Hill for over 20 years and often talked about putting something back into the area they loved before they finally started their own business. When they suddenly found themselves made redundant, they realised this was the opportunity they'd been waiting for. They'd been working on a business plan for nearly seven years, but it still took another year to secure the arch that would become Dugard & Daughters.

Tenacity, though, is part of what makes one business succeed where another fails. Rosie and Neil knew that the ethos had to be as right as the location. Dugard & Daughters was to be a place where their customers – many of whom they'd known for years from the local community – could buy everything they needed to make a good dinner; a place that combined the best elements of a traditional butchers and a larder.

A traditional approach holds sway on the butchery side. Whole carcasses are brought in to preserve the integrity of the meat, which is all English, rare-breed, and free-range sourced directly from the some of the UK's best breeders and small farms. Gloucester Old Spot pork from the Rare Breed Meat Company lines up alongside salt marsh lamb from Foulness Island in Essex, free-range chicken from Herb Fed Poultry and Fosse Meadows Farm and grass-fed beef from small cattle farms around the UK. The beef is carefully dry-aged to 4 weeks, with some ribs and loins being aged for up to 10 weeks, to give them a distinctive succulent tenderness and flavour.

Classic butcher's staples like charcuterie, oxtails, veal escalopes, and beef dripping and many more are back on the menu too, but the butchery works in balance with the 'larder' side of the title. It was the first shop in the area to stock organic vegetables; and after requests from customers began to stock freshly-baked bread from a local bakery. To round out the ingredients you need for a hearty meal, there are also pastas, teas, coffees, jams, honeys, biscuits, crispbreads, cheeses, condiments, and cordials sourced from the most flavoursome producers and suppliers. Oh, and Dugard & Daughters have reached out into South London's local craft brewers and makers to stock local beers and spirits too.

The proof of the pudding is certainly in the eating in the case of Dugard & Daughters and testament to the fact that the simplest ideas, done well with love and passion, are always the best!

Dugard & Daughters.

# Dugard & Daughters
# SALT MARSH LAMB RUMP WITH CHERRY TOMATOES

This is a favourite midweek dinner of ours. It's a quick 15-minute meal that's both super-tasty and super-healthy. We use salt marsh lamb – they graze on salt marshes making the meat really flavoursome and tender.

Preparation time including cooking: 12-15 minutes | Serves As many as you like!

## Ingredients

Salt marsh lamb rump, boned (allow 150-200g of lamb per person)

Organic tomatoes, cherry, preferably on the vine (allow 4 –6 per person)

Olive oil, to drizzle

Sea salt, coarse

Balsamic vinegar

## Method

Preheat the oven to 180°c and turn the grill onto a medium heat.

Place the cherry tomatoes in a baking tray, drizzle them with olive oil, sprinkle them with salt, and then finally drizzle over the balsamic vinegar.

Select a pan for the lamb that can go both on the hob and in the oven, put it on the hob on full heat. When it is at its hottest, add a little olive oil. Then, put the cherry tomatoes under the grill for 8-10 minutes or until nicely grilled.

Add the lamb rumps fat side down in the pan. Keep them fat side down for 20-30 seconds before turning and browning each side for roughly a further 20 seconds each before placing the pan in the preheated oven for 8 minutes.

Once done, take the pan out of the oven and transfer the lamb to a wooden chopping board to rest for a further 4-5 minutes.

To serve, simply plate up with the cherry tomatoes and enjoy!

(This dish also works well with new potatoes and seasonal greens; or sauerkraut; or beetroot!)

# Dugard & Daughters,
# 4-WEEK DRY-AGED RIB ROAST (WITH ALL THE TRIMMINGS!)

A real crowd pleaser, this dish is very versatile. A single rib will serve 2 or 3 people midweek while the 4 bone rib roast extravaganza can be dished up for a crowd. At Dugard & Daughters our beef is sourced from free-range, grass-fed, rare breed farms and then dry-aged onsite for at least 4 weeks for the best flavour.

Preparation time inc. cooking: 2 hours (To cook the beef medium rare calculate at 15 minutes per 454g plus an additional 15 minutes @ 180°c) | Serves 8

## Ingredients

**For the beef:**

3kg beef rib roast (preferably French trimmed 3 bone dry-aged)

Olive oil

3 red onions, medium

Salt

Pepper

**For the potatoes:**

1½kg potatoes (Maris Piper)

250-300g goose fat

Salt

**For the gravy:**

500ml beef stock

1 glass red wine

2 tsp mustard, whole grain

2 tbsp plain flour

Salt

Pepper

**For the cauliflower cheese:**

1 cauliflower (trim leaves and keep head)

100g plain flour

100g butter

350ml milk

400g cheddar cheese, strong

Salt

Pepper

## Method

Remove the beef from the fridge two hours before cooking. Preheat oven to 180°c, peel and halve the onions, add them with some olive oil and salt to the roasting tray, making sure the onions are well covered. Put to one side.

Place a heavy-bottomed pan on a high heat, rub olive oil and salt over the beef.

When the pan is smoking, place the beef in face-side down. Brown each side for 2 minutes and all over to a maximum of 10 minutes. Transfer the rib and juices to the roasting tray. Place this in the preheated oven and cook for as long as the formula above suggests.

When cooked, remove the beef from the oven, place on a chopping board to rest for 20 minutes before carving. Keep the roasting tray for the gravy.

Peel and cut the potatoes, add them to a pan of salted cold water. Leave for ten minutes then rinse in cold water. Repeat this twice before adding fresh water and salt and then bring the pan to the boil. Reduce to a simmer for around 10 minutes. While they're cooking, add the goose fat to a baking tray and heat in the oven. Draining the potatoes, shake in the pan to fluff up the edges before placing in the baking tray of piping hot goose fat. Making sure each is coated with fat, return to the oven for a further 1 hour 15 minutes, turn every 20 minutes to make sure each side is crisped.

For the cauliflower cheese, cut into florets and parboil for 8-12 minutes, drain and place in an oven-proof dish. Add the butter and plain flour to a saucepan over a low heat. Stir continuously until they form a paste. Turn the heat up, and add the milk, stirring until smooth. Grate in half the cheese, whisking to ensure the cheese is fully melted. Pour this over the cauliflower and grate the rest of the cheese on top. Place in a 200°c oven for 20 minutes.

To make the gravy, mix the plain flour with cold water in the beef roasting tray to make a runny paste and set aside. Place the roasting tray with the onions still in it on a high heat on your hob and bring it to a sizzle. Then, add a glass of red wine and reduce for 2 minutes before adding the beef stock and the mustard and stir well. Add the flour paste slowly until the desired thickness is achieved. Add salt and pepper to taste, but keep on the heat until the last moment so it's piping hot when served!

Plate up as desired, and serve immediately!

# *Our cups runneth* OVER

Dvine Cellar and Cellar.SW4 are making bibliophiles and casual wine-lovers alike sit up and take notice with their refreshing take on our favourite tipples...

Far more than we care to admit, we all have a tendency to be creatures of habit, going for what we know, rather than exploring the new. This extends to the wine we drink. We reach for the Rioja; we self-define as Pinot people because, well, that's what we've always drunk. Greg Andrews, owner of Dvine Cellar and Cellar.SW4 is on a mission to change our ingrained drinking habits.

Both outlets specialise in biodynamic, organic and sustainably-produced wines, with an emphasis on handcrafted varieties produced on family-run, lower-level production winemakers. Greg and his team focus on vineyards that have a real connection to their winemaking process; to their region; and to their location. With over 300 hundred wines drawn from around the globe in stock, the emphasis is on high-quality choice for the customer at every price point.

'Wine is our passion,' explains Greg. 'It isn't just about finding magnificent wines. Part of our job is to introduce them to customers and vice versa.'

To that end, Dvine Cellar works with customers to help find the perfect wine for events, meals, and menu choices through one-to-one engagement; events; and a full programme of tasting events. Customers not only get to try the hidden gems of the wine world; but also to experience that most perfect of gastronomic storms where the wine complements the food, unlocking both.

'We're primarily a retail outlet,' adds Greg. 'But our approach is winning us a strong corporate following in the City of London and beyond.'

It's also winning glowing reviews among the movers and shakers on London's bar scene as Cellar.SW4 builds on its sister outlet's strengths. This wine-bar and shop in nearby Clapham exudes laid-back elegance. The wine-list and menu alike again focus on the organic, sustainable, and bio-diverse. There's an antipodean slant to the wine, but the beers and ales reach out into the thriving local brewers to pull in great brews by Mondo Brewing Company; Brixton Brewery; and Gypsy Hill. Perfectly situated opposite Clapham High Street Overground for those on a night out; it's also building a great reputation for bespoke events, wine-tastings and pairings. If life without wine is unthinkable (and it is!), both places should be first on your list to visit and fall in love with.

# Cellar SW4

# FRENCH ONION & THREE CHEESE TOASTED SANDWICH

This French onion toasted sandwich isn't just any old toastie
– it encapsulates the great bar snack, an essential accompaniment
to any glass of wine.

Preparation time: 15 minutes | Cooking time: 40 minutes | Serves 4

## Ingredients

**For the French onion soup paste:**

500g onions, sliced

500g shallots, sliced

1 tsp garlic, finely chopped

50g butter

2 tbsp olive oil

½ tsp sugar

1 litre beef stock (you can replace this with vegetable boullion for a vegetarian alternative)

500ml white wine

Salt and pepper to taste

**To serve:**

Sourdough bread, 2 slices per sandwich

A large handful of grated Emmental cheese

A large handful of grated Comté cheese

A slice of Raclette cheese

Mayonnaise

Green leaf salad

## Method

### For the French onion soup paste

You can make the French onion soup paste ahead of time for convenience.

Place a large saucepan on a gentle heat. Add the oil, then the butter.

Add the sliced onions, shallots, garlic and sugar and cook until caramelised, this should take around 8-10 minutes. Once golden, reduce the heat and allow the onions to cook for a further 30 minutes to a dark caramelised nutty brown colour. Add the white wine and reduce. Gently scrape the pan to loosen the onions and dissolve the residue from the base of the pan.

Add the stock then turn up the heat to a rigorous simmer.

Cook until reduced to a paste, this should take around an hour until you have a chutney-like consistency. Remove from the heat and allow to cool.

The paste will keep for around 7 days in an air-tight container in the fridge with a dash of oil on top to seal. For the sandwich, ideally use a toasted sandwich grill or flat plate if you have one, alternatively heat up a heavy-based frying pan to around 180°c.

Spread the mayonnaise on the outside of your sliced sourdough bread – this creates a golden crust when cooked. Spread a heaped tablespoon of the French onion soup paste on the inside of one slice of the bread, then add the grated Emmental and Comté cheese. Finally place a slice of the Raclette cheese on top and then add the second slice of sourdough, with the mayonnaise on the outside.

### To serve

Place on a hot sandwich grill for 5 minutes until golden brown, the cheeses should be oozing.

Slice in half, and serve with a dressed green salad and a chilled glass of Chardonnay or Pinot.

# *Wine* RECOMMENDATIONS

A selection of tantalising-tipples paired
with some of our favourite dishes in the book.

## Aga's Little Deli

*Bermondsey Frier on Sourdough*

*Vouvray 'La Dilettante' Catherine at Pierre Breton, Loire Valley,
France*

The fruit-driven dry Vouvray will sit perfectly with the fried
spices.

## The Alma

*Refried Black Bean Tacos, Tomatillo Salsa, Avocado, Chargrilled
Corn*

*Holly's Garden Pinot Gris Gipsland, Australia*

Avocado and salsa need a bright fruit-driven dry white, and
this Pinot Gris is just that. An extremely bright white wine,
with tingly fruit flavours and a touch of honeyed almond.
Crisp and precise on the palate.

## B Street Deli

*Mixed Cheese and Charcuterie Board*

*Daphne, Cosimo Masini, Tuscany, Italy*

Cheese is often mismatched with heavy reds, and should really
be enjoyed with a textured white or fresh red (depending
on the cheeses). Daphne is an amber coloured skin contact
wine that has the structure to sit well beside both cheese and
charcuterie.

## Bell & Sons

*Mediterranean Rolled Porchetta*

*Raisins Gaulois, Marcel & Marie Lapierre, Beaujolais, France*

Pork needs a fresh buoyant red that isn't going to dominate
this lighter red meat. This Gamay has the fresh fruit to do this
and will have you reaching for another glass.

## Canopy Beer Co.

*Full Moon Porter Cake*

*'After 3' Monastrell Vino Dulce Natural, Casa Los Frailes,
Valencia, Spain*

This sweet Monastrell is a rare find that measures up perfectly
to chocolate. Deep, rich, vanilla-tinged fruit is a smooth joy
to finish any dinner.

## Cellar.SW4

*French Onion Toastie*

*Chardonnay, Sorrenberg, Beechworth, Australia*

The structure and comforting texture of this Chardonnay is
perfect with the Alpine cheese of Comté and Emmental. Its
nuttiness bonds well with the sourdough and caramelised
onion soup; a combination to savour.

## Chadwicks

*The Hobbit Pie*

*Mas Buscados, Tempranillo & Petit Verdot, La Mancha, Spain*

Fresh, moreish Tempranillo & Petit Verdot that has some
lively fruit notes with tons of damson and blackberry.

## Champor-Champor

*King River Prawns, Yellow Turmeric Curry, Egg, Cream, Celery*

*Gewurztraminer, Rolly Gasmann, Alsace, France*

This Gewurz is a sensational flavour bomb that yields honeyed
lychee and stone fruits, with a little spice to finish.

## Christopher's Bakery

*Dulwich Sourdough*

*Extra Dry NV, Pelegrim, Kent, England*

Our niche English sparkling is made using traditional
methods, the same way Champagne is made, so the fresh
acidity and yeasty notes will perfectly balance the sourdough.

Beck Ink

## Comfort & Joy
*Oven-Baked Falafels*
*Sauvignon Blanc, Dog Point, Marlborough, New Zealand*
This fragrant Sauvignon Blanc has enough tropical fruit zest and acidity to be sipped alongside the spicy falafels.

## Constancia
*Beef Empanadas*
*'U Turn' Malbec, Uco Valley, Argentina*
The dark fruit of Malbec coupled with this fresh wine-making approach will have you craving a second glass.

## Elvira's Secret Pantry
*Blueberry and Almond Tart*
*Pink Muscat, Stella Bella, Margaret River, Australia*
This modestly sparkling blush is a fun match with the sweet almond and blueberry flavours.

## Estate Office Coffee
*Killer Sausage Rolls*
*Lambrusco 'Marc Aurelio', Az.Ag. Crocizia*
Lambrusco is back! This party starter is a perfect aperitif and has enough fruit and 'refreshability' to live alongside the spicy sausage rolls.

## Flock and Herd
*Feather Blade and Ox Kidney Pie*
*Lo Petit Fantet, Corbierres France*
This biodynamic Corbierres delivers some bright juice with a soft tannic structure that will sit nicely alongside this wholesome pie.

## Flotsam & Jetsam
*Lemon Meringue Cake*
*Muscat De Saint-Jean, Clos du Gravillas, Languedoc France*
A delicate Muscat that is fresh enough and fruity enough to balance the lemony sweetness.

## Franklins Restaurant and Farm Shop
*Rabbit, Cider and Bacon*
*La Clos Blanc de Vougeot, Domaine de la Vougeraie, Burgundy, France*
An epic Chardonnay with its very modest barrel aging and purity will harmonise with the rabbit and bacon.

## The Habit
*Courgette, Vine Tomato, Basil and Almond Lasagne*
*'SP68' Occhipinti, Sicily, Italy*
Arianna Occhipinti has been making wine since she was sixteen years old, and this textured wine led by citrus is a perfect counter for the lasagne.

## The Inkspot Brewery/Art & Craft
*St Johns' Brisket*
*'The Unforgettable' Grenache Syrah Mataro, Langhorne Creek, Australia*
Brilliant with beef, this well-rounded drinker delivers abundant fruit with some chocolate and spice.

## The Inkspot Brewery/Art & Craft
*Smoked Goose Leg with Smoked Tomato Beans*
*Priorat, Vi de Vila Porreira, Priorat, Spain*
Priorat has the tannin and acidity to stand up to the lusciousness of goose meat. The darker fruits and spice will temper this dish beautifully.

## London Smoke & Cure
*Smoked Duck Breast and Lentil With Cherry*
*Beck Ink Weingut Judith Beck, Burgenland, Austria*
Deep and dark cherry fruits come to the fore, but also have the acidity to balance out the protein and earthiness of the lentils.

## Olley's Fish Experience
*Grilled Salmon and Salad*
*MA'D Tokaji Dry Furmint, Tokaji, Hungary*
Salmon needs acidity to combat its heavier flavour, and the Ma'd Dry Furmint delivers this with green apricot and nectarine fruits, but a very dry backbone.

## Piccalilli Caff
*Aubergine Eggs in Purgatory*
*Soli Pinot, Thracian Valley Bulgaria*
A light red is often great with eggs. This pinot has a flavour of earthy wild strawberries, and is bright enough to live up to the eggs and aubergine, but fruity enough to deal with the spice.

## Piccalilli Caff
*Moroccan Orange Cake*
*Torrontes Tardio, Familia Zuccardi, Mendoza, Argentina*
A perfumed, light dessert wine with tangerine and apricot hints.

## Piccalilli Caff
*Scotch Egg*
*Blanc de Franc Pet Nat, Jamsheed, Victoria, Australia*
This Cabernet Franc Pet Nat (mildly sparkling) rosé delivers a fruity fizz that will embellish the egg and spiced pork.

# Sweet
# SECRETS

An artisan Italian micro-bakery in South-east London, Elvira's Secret Pantry is dedicated to making bespoke and 'free-from' sweet and savoury delights – gluten-free, dairy-free and yeast-free, as well as vegan.

What do you do when you love baking but are intolerant to gluten and dairy? It can be difficult to find truly delicious baked treats that are free-from both of these common allergens. This was the dilemma that set Elvira on the course to starting up her flourishing business four years ago.

Elvira was working in arts management before launching Elvira's Secret Pantry. She found baking to be the ideal escape from the day-to-day stresses of her job, and was always trying out new gluten, dairy and yeast-free recipes in her spare time.

The first step towards transforming her passion into a business was a council-run course, where she learnt the ins and outs of setting up a market business in London. Elvira's Secret Pantry began life as a stall at Deptford market, and over the next few months and years, the business grew organically. Other markets followed – she became a popular trader at Crystal Palace and Beckenham markets, amongst others around South-east London.

Her Italian bakery specialises in family recipes with a twist of creativity, and her individuality soon led to her receiving wholesale orders from coffee shops, restaurants and independent retailers who loved her bespoke approach that enabled her to accommodate each customer. "I do everything myself," she explains, "so I can tailor a cake or bread or quiche to very specific needs."

As well as fulfilling many wholesale orders, Elvira also sells her products online. She puts the popularity of her fare down to her simple approach of using seasonal, organic and additive-free ingredients. "I only bake things that I love myself," Elvira admits, which means that her passion for flavour comes across in every bite.

The latest addition to Elvira's Secret Pantry comes in the form of her cooking classes. These can take place in her kitchen or in customer's own homes. Whether she is teaching how to make one of her favourite cakes (think lemon and poppy seed polenta cake), a quiche, fresh pasta or artisan bread, the classes always have an informal and friendly atmosphere.

With her wholesale orders continually increasing, demand for personal orders popping through on her website and a plethora of classes in the diary, it looks like Elvira's Secret Pantry might not be so secret any more.

# *Elvira's Secret Pantry*
# BLUEBERRY AND ALMOND TART

Delicious shortcrust pastry with a nutty and fruity filling.

Preparation time: 30 minutes, plus resting | Cooking time: 1 hour 15 minutes | Serves 8

## Ingredients

**For the sweet shortcrust pastry:**

350g gluten-free self-raising flour

60g unrefined golden caster sugar

150 dairy-free spread

2 medium organic egg yolks

1 medium organic egg, plus 1 egg, beaten, for sealing

**For the filling:**

85g dairy-free spread

155g unrefined golden caster sugar

1 lemon, zested

175g ground almonds

2 medium organic eggs

250g fresh blueberries

50g almond flakes

## Method

You will need a 23cm/9 inch fluted loose-bottomed flan tin.

To make the pastry, measure the flour, sugar and spread into a food processor. Whiz until the mixture looks like breadcrumbs and then add the egg yolks and egg. Whiz again until it forms a ball. Wrap it in cling film and put it into the fridge to rest for at least half an hour.

Preheat the oven to 190°c/fan 170°c. Using your hands, gently press the pastry into the edges and ridges of the greased tart tin. Line with non-stick baking paper and fill with baking beans. Blind bake in the preheated oven for 10 minutes.

Take out of the oven and remove the baking beans and paper. Return the empty pastry shell to the oven for another 8 minutes. Take out of the oven, brush the pastry with a beaten egg to seal it, and bake for another 8 minutes. Set aside to cool.

In the meantime, prepare the filling by beating together the spread, sugar and zest until it is light and fluffy. Stir in the ground almonds and eggs. Add half the blueberries and spoon into the pastry case. Smooth the top using the back of a metal spoon, then scatter over the remaining blueberries and press them in lightly. Scatter over the almond flakes.

Bake for 40-45 minutes until the filling is golden and feels firm to the touch. Cool the tart for 10 minutes in the tin, then lift onto a serving plate. Serve warm or at room temperature.

### Cook's tip

Roll what's left of the pastry to make little tart cases. Pop in a spoonful of jam and bake for 20-30 minutes.

# *Speciality* COFFEE

From its unusual premises to its artisan coffee, Estate Office Coffee has brought a refreshing change to coffee lovers in Streatham.

It may sound like an unusual name for a coffee shop, but Estate Office Coffee takes its name from its curious setting – a 1906 estate office that served the neighbouring residential mansion blocks. Over the last century, the estate office has served as everything from a high-class laundry before the war to a money transfer shop in recent years.

It is owned by coffee fanatic Joe Thomas. A Streatham local, he had become more and more obsessed with coffee over the last five years, and was travelling to Balham every day to get his hands on his favourite brew. It was here he met barista and fellow coffee enthusiast Clark Griffin, and the pair decided to join forces to bring great coffee to Streatham.

Stumbling upon the premises happened in a serendipitous moment. When walking down the street one day Joe happened to see an estate agent putting a board in the empty estate office. "Without even breaking my stride, I walked straight in," says Joe, "and within a few weeks, the lease was signed."

Joe put his interior design career to good use to renovate the space. Reclaimed hardwood worktops came from an old school science lab, and a local welder made the legs. All the signage was painstakingly hand-gilded by a local artist. "We put the emphasis on three things: quality, integrity and workmanship," explains Joe, "and these apply to everything from the interior design to the food and coffee." He firmly believes in making everything the very best it can be.

With Clark as manager and head barista, and coffee sourced from Dalston-based Allpress Coffee, they were on track to bring a whole new coffee experience to Streatham. The mouth-watering array of cakes and pastries on the counter complements the drinks selection, and they have freshly made bread and homemade sausage rolls on offer too.

The cosy space has become a favourite haunt for locals who have made Estate Office Coffee a real community hub. As Clark and Joe both have small children themselves, they love to welcome families – in fact they know most of their regulars by their name (and their order!) by now. A true local gem, Estate Office Coffee is now an integral part of Streatham life.

# Estate Office Coffee
# KILLER SAUSAGE ROLLS

Our Killer Sausage Rolls started off as a Saturday special, but quickly became a permanent feature on the menu. In a world of super-healthy snacks (which we love by-the-way) it's nice to offer an indulgent honest 'have a lie down afterwards' treat. That's these beauties. We love to enjoy them with plenty of mustard; English or American.

Preparation time: 30 minutes | Cooking time: 30 minutes | Makes 4 large, or 8 small

## Ingredients

1 sheet of pre-rolled puff pastry (life is too short to make your own)

450g premium quality sausage meat

1 large carrot, grated

120g hard goat's cheese, grated

100g red onion chutney

10g fresh sage, chopped

40g fine breadcrumbs

1 medium egg, beaten

## Method

Preheat the oven to 210°c/190°c fan. Lay out the sheet of puff pastry and cut it in half to give two equal squares.

Place the sausage meat into a large bowl. Add the grated carrot, cheese, chutney and half the sage, and combine well. Divide the sausage meat mix into two and roll each half into a cylinder shape to the same width as a pastry square.

Lay out one of the pastry squares and place one cylinder of the sausage meat mix on the pastry sideways, 1 inch from the edge closest to you. Egg wash the edge of the pastry square furthest away from you. Now it's time to roll it all up.

Start with the inch edge of the pastry closest to you, fold it up and then roll it up until you have reached the end of the sheet. You should now have something which resembles a long sausage roll.

Repeat with the other sausage meat cylinder and pastry square. Once you have two large rolls, cut each in half to give four large sausage rolls. Divide again if you want to make eight smaller ones.

Combine the remaining sage with the breadcrumbs. Cut some baking parchment and place on a baking tray. Using baking parchment isn't essential but helps with minimising washing-up later. Place the sausage rolls (with the edge/seam on the bottom) on to the baking tray. Brush each sausage roll with egg wash and sprinkle over the breadcrumb mixture. Place on to the middle shelf of the preheated oven and bake for 30 minutes.

Enjoy!

# Antipodean
# EATING

Independent café Flotsam & Jetsam brings a taste of the Antipodean way of life to Wandsworth Common.

Owned by New Zealander Hana, Flotsam & Jetsam is a laid-back café that offers an opportunity to enjoy the warmth associated with dining down under. When she moved to London, Hana's favourite way to explore the city was venturing to different neighbourhoods and trying out local eateries.

Inspired by the array of independent cafés peppering South London, Hana decided she wanted to open her own Antipodean-style café. She spent months looking for the perfect location, before finally discovering her dream premises in August 2014.

The next few months were spent doing a complete refurb, which, to Hana's delight, revealed numerous original features. When she discovered the beautiful parquet floor she was over the moon, as it worked perfectly with the exposed brick walls they had painstakingly stripped back. Architect husband Bradley helped with the stunning design, featuring plenty of eye-catching features on which customers always comment.

In 2015 Flotsam & Jetsam opened its doors and was soon a favourite in its diverse community. The family-friendly café has baby changing facilities and a flexible children's menu – if they've got the ingredients, they'll whip something up to please your little ones. Situated on the common, it is also

dog-friendly – in fact it's a popular spot for a post-dog-walk brunch.

The menu is vibrant, nutritious and tasty – think freshly made porridge with toppings that change according to the seasons, Bircher muesli with homemade coconut yoghurt, or smashed avocado and feta on sourdough. There are plenty of not-quite-so-healthy treats, too, such as American pancakes with all the toppings.

They make everything in-house, from jams and curds to focaccia and cornbread. Hana's mum, Stephanie, is a pastry chef and her creations adorn the cake display. Her banana bread has acquired a loyal following, along with the famous Anzac biscuits.

Although Hana uses local suppliers for most of her produce, there are a few essential ingredients from further afield. Pic's peanut butter is one of these, in fact she even sells it in the café. She also serves Allpress Coffee from New Zealand and T2 tea from Australia.

Flotsam & Jetsam takes its name from curious things that wash up on shore, inspired not only by the New Zealand love of the water that surrounds it, but by the gems they have uncovered along the way.

# Flotsam & Jetsam
# LEMON MERINGUE CAKE

This citrusy meringue cakes makes a delicious change from the usual lemon meringue pie. Light sponge, a zingy lemon curd filling and a sweet meringue topping are a match made in heaven – perfect with a cup of T2 tea!

Preparation time: 1 hour | Cooking time: 1 hour | Serves 8

## Ingredients

### For the cake:

315g plain flour

15g baking powder

8g salt

5 eggs

300ml buttermilk or plain Greek yoghurt

150ml flavourless oil, e.g. grapeseed, sunflower

300g caster sugar

3 lemons, zested

8ml vanilla essence

### For the lemon curd filling:

3g gelatine powder

1 tbsp cold water

1 egg

65g caster sugar

1 lemon, zested and juiced

75g butter

### For the meringue topping:

2 egg whites

100g caster sugar

## Method

### For the cake

Line a 20cm round cake tin. Preheat the oven to 170°c (fan). Sift the flour, baking powder and salt into a bowl. In a separate bowl, mix together the eggs, yoghurt/buttermilk, oil, sugar, lemon zest and vanilla. Fold the wet ingredients into the dry ingredients, then pour into the lined cake tin. Bake for 1 hour, then leave to cool. Once cooled, slice the cake in half horizontally, ready to fill with the lemon curd.

### For the lemon curd filling

Mix the gelatine powder into the cold water to hydrate. Use a stick blender to blitz the egg. In a saucepan, place the sugar, lemon juice and lemon zest, stir and heat. Add the egg to the mixture once warm, and continue stirring until the mixture thickens and bubbles appear. Remove from the heat. Cut the butter into cubes and blitz into the curd mixture while hot. Blitz the hydrated gelatine into the curd mixture. Refrigerate the filling until cooled, then blitz one more time to remove any lumps. Spread lemon curd onto one of the cake halves and top with the second cake half.

### For the meringue topping

In a metal bowl set over hot water, heat the egg whites with the sugar, whisking gently while it warms. Heat until just above body temperature, then transfer to the bowl of a stand mixer fitted with the whisk attachment. Beat on high speed until the mixture becomes thick and stiff. Transfer the mixture to a piping bag with a plane nozzle attachment. Pipe dots of meringue over top of cake until it is completely covered. Flame the meringue to brown lightly – use a blowtorch or place it under a hot grill for a short time. Alternatively, leave the meringue white.

# *Customers* FLOCKING

On thriving Bellenden Road in Peckham, Flock and Herd is a dynamic young butchery who pack an inspiring collection of meat into their South London shop.

Since it opened five years ago, Flock and Herd has been attracting queues down the street thanks to its impressive choice of free-range, rare-breed and locally sourced meat. Approachable, accessible and welcoming, this is a butchery for everyone who simply loves to cook great meat.

Charlie Shaw trained to be a butcher ten years ago, before gaining experience cutting meat for some of London's most famous restaurants. Passionate about food, cooking and meat in particular, he decided to open his own butchery five years ago in the heart of Peckham's bustling Bellenden Road. The shop became home to a small team of young, passionate butchers, who took pride in sourcing some of the finest meat in the capital.

Doing the sourcing themselves meant they could search for the best farmers around and work closely with them to ensure the highest quality produce. Being a small but growing butchery has enabled them to travel around the Home Counties to not only meet their suppliers, but to build up close relationships with them.

From English veal to seasonal game, Flock and Herd can be flexible with the produce they sell, reacting to the changing seasons and offering local customers the best of beef, lamb, pork and poultry, as well as wild boar and venison, for example.

As well as fresh cuts of meat, they also make a wide range of sausages, burgers, koftas and meatballs, and they cure their own bacon – the treacle back bacon is one of their most popular products. They also push the boundaries with a mouth-watering selection of dry rubs and marinades – they really try to do as much as they can in the small space they have available. The Melton Mowbray pork pies have developed a loyal following, sourced directly from Charlie's friend in Melton Mowbray.

Being a food-loving team, they can offer advice to customers on cooking techniques, such as cooking times and what cuts are best for what style of cooking. They will also be able to tell you about the provenance of the meat you buy. Open Tuesday to Saturday every week, Flock and Herd are on-hand for quick dinners, summer barbecues, impressive joints and those all-important breakfast goodies.

Keep up to date with their latest developments on Twitter and Instagram @flockandherd.

# Flock and Herd
# FEATHER BLADE & OX KIDNEY PIE

Using the best-quality feather blade, ox kidney, streaky bacon
and bone marrow provides beautiful depth of flavour
and contrasting textures in this warming pie.

Preparation time: 1 hours | Cooking time: 4 hours | Serves 6-8

## Ingredients

### For the filling:

1.75kg feather blade, diced into 2½cm cubes

2 large onions, finely diced

1 tsp smoked paprika

2 sprigs dried rosemary

Pinch dried thyme

3 bay leaves

Pinch celery salt

500g smoked streaky bacon or pancetta, diced

300g ox kidney

1 shaft of bone marrow

3 garlic cloves, finely diced

Knob of butter, plus extra for greasing

660ml ale of your choice

350ml beef stock

Salt and pepper

Olive oil, for cooking

### For the suet pastry:

300g finely grated beef suet

550g self-raising flour, sifted

275ml cold water

Salt and pepper

Beaten egg, for egg washing

## Method

Preheat the oven to 180°c. Meanwhile, warm a little olive oil in a large frying pan and brown the meat, bacon, kidney and bone marrow in batches. Set the meat aside in a heavy-bottomed casserole dish.

Using the same frying pan that you used to brown the meat, sauté the onions, rosemary, thyme and bay leaves. Season with celery salt and cook until they are golden. Add the pancetta, ox kidneys, the bone marrow shaft, the garlic and a knob of butter, and fry for a further minute.

Combine the onions, beef and smoked paprika in the casserole dish. Add the ale and stock, cover with a lid and cook in the oven or on the hob for 3½ hours or until the stock has reduced by half.

Once the meat is tender and the gravy has reduced, set aside.

To make the pastry, combine the suet and sifted flour in a large mixing bowl, adding the water to make a soft dough. Season slightly. The dough should be firm and not sticking to the hands as it is mixed.

Roll the pastry out on a slightly flour-dusted surface to the shape of the chosen pie dish. Butter the bottom of the dish and lay the pastry in.

Once the meat has completely cooled (it is very important to let the meat cool completely as this will stop the pastry bottom becoming soggy) pour it into the dish, positioning the marrow shaft in the centre. Egg wash the edges and lay the pastry lid on top, cutting a cross to allow the marrow to slip through and crimp to seal.

Preheat the oven to 200°c and then cook the pie in the oven 15 minutes or until it is golden in colour.

# Farm to FORK

Two gastronomic institutions at the heart of East Dulwich,
Franklins Restaurant and Farm Shop have been putting British food
at the heart of their business for nearly two decades.

A beloved fixture of SE22's food scene, Franklins is situated on bustling Lordship Lane, in two units either side of the junction with Bawdale Road. The restaurant itself was the original arm of the business, set up by Tim Sheehan and Rod Franklin 18 years ago.

Inspired by our country's produce, Franklins Restaurant became known for its British-oriented approach and its daily changing menus. From the outset, they wanted to buy as much as possible direct from British farms and source all of their fish from British waters.

18 years later and the ethos remains unchanged, although the restaurant has evolved with the changing times. The bar area at the front is a haven for craft beer lovers, gin enthusiasts and wine aficionados, providing the perfect ambience for a pre-dinner aperitif or a post-work drink. Everything they serve in the restaurant is made in-house and from scratch, be that the bread for the soup or the crackers for the cheese. They also love pickling and curing to make the most of seasonal ingredients.

As they became known for their farm-fresh local produce, people began asking to buy ingredients from them, so, when the neighbouring unit became available ten years ago, they decide to open it as a shop to sell the same ingredients they used in the restaurant kitchen. Today it is a treasure trove of local and seasonal goodies, with fruits and veggies from community growers and local farms.

"We try to respond to demand", explains Tim, "so the products vary depending on what customers tell us they want to buy, as well as what is available seasonally." Open seven days a week, Franklins Farm Shop is a go-to shop for many people in the area – some of whom have been shopping there for the last decade.

Both the shop and the restaurant, which, by their very nature are intrinsically linked, have become much-loved fixtures on Lordship Lane. The thriving restaurant and bustling shop have become hubs of the local community – putting seasonality on the restaurant menu as well as on people's tables at home.

# Franklins
# RABBIT, CIDER & BACON

This is delicious served with some creamy mashed potatoes
or some fresh spring vegetables.

Preparation time: 20 minutes | Cooking time: 1 hour 30 minutes | Serves 4

## Ingredients

1 farmed or wild rabbit

2 tbsp plain flour

2 tbsp mustard powder

4 streaky bacon rashers, cut into
lardons

1 onion, chopped

1 carrot, chopped

4 garlic cloves, crushed

1 bottle of good cider

250ml chicken stock

1 bunch of thyme

2 bay leaves

Salt and pepper

Oil and butter, for cooking

Spring vegetables or mashed potatoes,
to serve

## Method

Portion the rabbit – you can get your butcher to do this for you. Mix together the flour and mustard powder, then dust the rabbit with it.

Splash some oil into a heavy pan and place over the heat. Brown the rabbit pieces in the hot pan, then remove from the pan and set aside. Add a knob of butter to your pan, then throw in the chopped bacon, onion and carrot, and sweat until a nice golden colour.

Add the garlic, then pour in the cider and bubble for a few minutes. Add the stock, thyme and bay, and simmer for 10 minutes. Add the rabbit pieces back into the pan, cover and simmer gently for an hour – the rabbit should be nice and tender. Season to taste.

You can sieve the sauce or leave it chunky. Serve with some nice spring vegetables or some mash.

# Manning THE FORT

Although down from their peak numbers in the Victorian era, there are still thousands of pubs in London so you have to be good to survive, thrive and stand out. Bermondsey's The Garrison gastro-pub, though, seems to do it effortlessly. Their killer combination of a great location at the heart of one of London's burgeoning foodie hubs and a well-deserved reputation for good food, good drink and a good atmosphere has made it a go-to destination.

Part of Mosaic's Pub and Dining Group, The Garrison reflects their belief that every pub should let its own identity shine through. The frontage's mix of old-school charm with a modern feel is reflected throughout – this is a space that's at once welcoming and relaxing. There's a light airy feel to the main room that's beautifully balanced by the intimacy of the underground cinema room, available for business meetings, a lunch with friends or private hire.

The care and attention to detail carries through to the menu. The emphasis is on using and serving high-quality produce sourced from local suppliers and British farms and fishermen to an informed clientele, and a selection that's regularly updated to reflect the best of what's available. The Garrison can do classic pub staples too. After all, their take on the great British pork pie (a delicious combination of pork shoulder, smoked streaky shoulder, smoked streaky bacon, pork belly, mace, ground white pepper, garlic powder, nutmeg and cumin) beat off all-comers to win Action Against Hunger's inaugural pie-off!

But there's a lightness of touch and shrewd judge of flavour combinations and ingredients on offer too. The Devon Crab risotto with samphire, pea shoots, and lemon oil is a wonderful combination of comfort food and zesty delight, for example, while Saturday's 'Bottomless Brunch' menu, including a delicious-sounding Smoked Haddock with poached eggs, rosti potatoes and hollandaise actually make foregoing the lie-in and getting up in the morning the right option!

Don't just take our word for it as The Garrison has placed highly in Travel Mag's recent review of the ten best places to eat south of the river, where its breakfast, brunch, lunch and dinner menus were described as perfect 'for any time of the day' – something that its growing number of repeat and new customers attests to.

Frankly, a good gastro-pub with bags of charm, bags of character and bags of the good stuff when it comes to flavour are hard to find. In The Garrison, however, we've definitely found one!

# PAN-FRIED COD, CRISP CHORIZO AND COURGETTE CAKE WITH ROMESCO SAUCE

This dish has become one of our favourites here at the Garrison, both in the kitchen and among our customers. The chorizo and smoky Romesco sauce bring a Spanish influence to the dish, which pairs wonderfully with the delicate fresh flavour of North Atlantic Cod and the courgette cake.

Preparation time: 15 minutes | Cooking time: 45 minutes | Serves 4

## Ingredients

**For the crispy chorizo:**

100g chorizo sausage

½ shallot

2 thyme sprigs

**For the courgette cake (quiche):**

2 courgettes

70g ricotta

2 tbsp Parmesan cheese

Splash of lemon oil

1 egg

3 tbsp ground almonds

Salt & pepper

**For the Romesco sauce:**

1 red pepper

2 tbsp smoked, semi-dried tomatoes

1 tsp garlic purée

65g ground almonds

2 tomatoes

1 tbsp tomato purée

2 tbsp sherry vinegar

1 tsp smoked paprika

50ml extra virgin olive oil

Salt & pepper

**For the cod:**

4 x 150g cod fillets, skin on

Plain flour, for dusting

## Method

Cut the chorizo into small half centimetre cubes and slice the shallot thinly and then fry both together with a splash of oil until crispy, finishing with the thyme sprigs. Put to one side.

To make the courgette cake, grate the courgette and then mix it thoroughly with the other ingredients. Lining a suitable pan with baking parchment, fill it with the mixture before baking in a preheated oven at 155°c for 25 minutes before setting aside to cool. When it has cooled, carefully remove the cake from the pan and the parchment without breaking it.

Then, slice into individual portions and put to one side.

To make the Romesco sauce, roast the pepper until it is charring and caramelised, alongside the tomatoes. Allowing both to cool so that you can handle them, peel the pepper's skin and core before blending all the ingredients in a food processor, adding salt and pepper to taste.

Turning your attention to the cod, dust the skin with flour and then pan fry with a splash of oil for no more than 2 minutes (skin side down first) in a hot pan. Remove the pan with the fillets and place in the oven to finish for 5 minutes.

Add the courgette cake to a separate frying pan and cook with a little olive oil until their colour begins to develop, which should take no more then 2-3 minutes.

### To serve

Spread the Romesco sauce across a dining plate. Place a portion of courgette cake and a cod fillet so that they overlap, and then garnish with the crispy chorizo. Serve immediately.

# Organic GIN

From part-time hobby to Tooting's favourite tipple, Graveney Gin is produced in small batches, is totally organic and utterly delicious.

Graveney Gin is the one-woman enterprise of gin-enthusiast Victoria Christie. What began as a simple hobby is now, just a couple of years later, one of Tooting's fastest-growing independent businesses.

Victoria always dreamed of making gin. She started experimenting at home using a 5-litre still in the evenings after work, and began sharing her project on social media. It didn't take long for Tooting to take hold of it – people really loved the idea of having a gin made right there in their own neighbourhood.

Two years ago, Victoria was given the opportunity to launch her gin at a local festival. Armed with 200 bottles (which had taken her an eternity to make using her 5-litre still, as well as hand-bottling and hand-labelling every single one), Victoria launched Graveney Gin. After a whirlwind day – involving her husband dashing home to label more bottles as stock ran out – Victoria was overwhelmed at the local response to her gin… there was no going back from here.

The gin is special, not only because it is made locally in South London, but because it reflects Victoria herself and what she loves in life. The gin is certified organic, uses fresh botanicals, and is hand-crafted in the truest sense. Graveney Gin donates 10% of its profits to a conservation charity that protects rare mountain gorillas in The Democratic Republic of Congo, a charity close to Victoria's heart.

In 2016, Victoria was offered a unit in Tooting Market. With budgets scribbled on a Nando's napkin, Victoria took the plunge to leave her job and concentrate on Graveney Gin full time. A magnificent crowd-funding effort followed, and with the help of Tooting residents, Victoria opened a nano bar in the corner of Tooting Market for people to taste her gin.

Today Victoria has a team running the bar for her, so that she can get back to her distillery in Merton Abbey Mills where she does everything from making the gin in her two 30-litre stills and hand-labelling the bottles to bookkeeping and marketing.

The most important thing to Victoria is customer feedback, especially since the business has been so whole-heartedly backed by the community. However, with a silver award at the International Spirit Competition 2016 under its belt, Graveney Gin's fame is spreading much further afield than its Tooting home.

Graveney Gin

# GRAVENEY GIN

GIN
THIS
WAY

ORGANIC

BORN IN · TOOTING

GRAVENEY
GIN

inspired by the pure love of gin

# Graveney Gin
## AMAZON

Choosing these two recipes for Graveney Gin were easy. The favourite amongst the bar with our customers is the Amazon, so it's a firm favourite and so easy to impress with at home.

Preparation time: 2 minutes | Serves 1

## Ingredients

*50ml Graveney Gin*

*200ml ginger beer*

*Slices of cucumber, to garnish*

## Method

Add the gin and ginger beer to a large Spanish gin and tonic glass. Garnish with the strips of cucumber and serve.

# Graveney Gin
## FRENCH 75

The French 75 is by far one of my personal favourites. It has the balance of sweet and sour, mixed with gin and Champagne – what's not to love.

Preparation time: 5 minutes | Serves 1

## Ingredients

45ml Graveney Gin

15ml freshly squeezed lemon juice

7½ml star syrup

75ml Champagne, cava or prosecco

Lemon zest twist, to garnish

## Method

Shake the gin, lemon juice and star syrup with ice in a cocktail shaker. Strain into a chilled glass and top with your choice of bubbles. Garnish with a lemon zest twist.

# *Modern British* BISTRO

Following the success of its first eatery in Nunhead,
The Habit is now also bringing fresh, simple and delicious
dishes to South London Gallery in Peckham, too.

The idea for The Habit was devised in 2015, a joint venture of South London local Dan Benjamins and chef John Hollins. John had built up his culinary reputation while working for Adam Byatt at Trinity Restaurant, Clapham. Like Dan, he wanted to open a neighbourhood bistro that would serve a whole range of food to the community – from the simplest breakfasts to more creative lunches.

They launched The Habit Nunhead in February 2016 with a simple ethos of serving fresh, seasonal and locally sourced food. They use local butchers who source their meat from Kent farmers, fruit and vegetables from nearby allotments or growers, and recently they have begun roasting their own coffee. They can boast being the only place to serve beers from Ignition Brewery in Lewisham, an ambitious social enterprise that employs people with learning disabilities.

The second venue followed in July 2017 in the gorgeous South London Gallery, a space that is close to the heart of owner Dan, who was born and bred in the area and whose parents attended Camberwell College of Arts right next door.

Dan and John work together to plan the regularly changing menu, which follows the seasons and is inspired by the bounty of produce on their doorstep. For breakfast, the options range from the delicious simplicity of fresh sourdough with butter and preserves to something more luxurious, such as crushed avocado, grilled courgette and poached egg on sourdough.

Lunch again spans the range from total simplicity to more substantial options. Seasonal soup is served with sourdough, as is the butterbean hummus and mixed olives. For something a little more special, there are various salads and a 28 day-aged beef burger. On Sunday, attention turns to the famous Habit roast, served from 12-5pm with all the trimmings.

The Nunhead venue opens for dinner on Friday and Saturday nights, something which Dan and John aim to expand to their Peckham venue too. They also host popular supper clubs and offer their versatile spaces out for events of all types. Being opposite the register office, they have hosted many a wedding reception, but are also a popular spot for birthday parties and other events, adapting their menus to suit any occasion.

Life is
change!

Sam Porritt
2010
Laser print with hand drawn elements in ac
200gsm acid free paper
Edition of 174, each edition is unique and co
of two A3 sheets, signed and numbered (un
£72 – £208.80 (SLG Fan Price £64.80 – £1

The Habit
CAFE & ESPRESSO BAR

INFO@THEHABITLOND
WWW.T

# *The Habit*
# COURGETTE, VINE TOMATO, BASIL AND ALMOND LASAGNE

This is a flavoursome vegetable lasagne that layers yellow and green courgettes with homemade tomato passata and homemade almond pesto.

Preparation time: 30 minutes | Cooking time: 30 minutes | Serves 4-6

## *Ingredients*

**For the passata:**

2 shallots, finely sliced

1kg cherry vine tomatoes

200ml red wine vinegar

50g soft brown sugar

½ pint water

2 garlic cloves, peeled and crushed

100% rapeseed oil, for cooking

**For the pesto:**

100g flaked almonds

2 bunches of basil

1 clove of garlic, peeled

50ml 100% rapeseed oil

**To assemble:**

2 yellow courgettes, thinly sliced on a mandoline

3 green courgettes, thinly sliced on a mandoline

A generous lump of Parmesan

## *Method*

### For the passata

Sweat off the shallots in a saucepan with a couple glugs of 100% rapeseed oil over a medium heat for 3-4 minutes until soft (do not allow them to colour).

Add the tomatoes, vinegar, sugar and water to the saucepan, then bring to a gentle simmer. Continue to cook and reduce down until the mixture resembles a jam consistency. At this point add the crushed garlic and remove the pan from the heat. Set aside to cool.

### For the pesto

Preheat the oven to 180°c, place the flaked almonds on a baking tray and lightly toast in the oven for 10 minutes. Add the toasted almond flakes to a small food processor or stick blender pot along with the remaining pesto ingredients. Blitz until you have a pesto texture.

### To assemble

Preheat the oven to 175°c. We're ready to build! Simply lay a piece of greaseproof paper in the base and up the sides of a smallish baking tray. Lay the sliced courgettes on the base, followed by passata with a couple of spoons of pesto. Finish with a generous grating of Parmesan. Repeat this until you have a full tray, making sure to lay the courgette slices in opposite ways for each layer.

Bake in the preheated oven for 30 minutes and serve with salads of your choice.

# *English gin*
# TRADITIONS

With gin undergoing a huge renaissance in the UK, Hayman's Gin
reminds us that their family have been making English gin
in the traditional way for over 150 years...

The Hayman family's history of distilling a true English Gin goes back all the way to 1863. The story begins with Christopher Hayman's great-grandfather, James Burrough, a pharmacist with a curiosity for medicinal ingredients, cordials and, most importantly, gin. He began distilling gin in 1863 on Cale Street in London – and that coveted gin recipe, which he scribbled in his notebook, is still in use by the family today.

Today Christopher is joined by his son James and daughter Miranda, and together they share the generations-old passion for producing true English gin in the traditional way.

Every gin is made by hand to original recipes in the traditional copper pot "Marjorie" – named after Christopher's mother. From the classic botanicals (juniper, coriander, lemon peel, orange peel, angelica root, cinnamon, cassia bark, orris root, liquorice and nutmeg) to the careful distillation process, Hayman's Gin is quite unique in that it follows a very traditional method that is particular to making a true English Gin.

Hayman's have returned to their London roots and their new distillery is in Balham, a stone's throw from their original home in Chelsea. Hayman's London Dry Gin (the popular choice for a G&T) is their award-winning, signature style. The 150-year-old family recipe includes a two-day distillation process, which the Hayman's insist isn't just used out of a sense of duty for tradition, but because it simply produces better gin. The first day sees the ten botanicals steeped in English wheat spirit, before the gin is distilled by hand in the copper pot still. This style of gin came into its own in the 19th and 20th centuries thanks to it being ideally suited to cocktails – not to mention being the perfect pairing for tonic.

The flagship Hayman's London Dry Gin is joined by Hayman's Old Tom Gin, a Victorian style of gin which predates the London Dry style, and the perfectly balanced Hayman's Sloe Gin, which is made from English sloe berries steeped in Hayman's London Dry Gin for 3-4 months.

The collection is completed with the cask-rested Family Reserve and the navy-strength Royal Dock, both of which continue to showcase Hayman's dedication to the time-honoured traditions of true English gin.

Hayman's Gin

# HAYMAN'S ENGLISH GIN & TONIC

This is the classic G&T.
(It should be served in a traditional English high ball glass).

Preparation time: 2 minutes | Serves 1

## Ingredients

Cubed ice

50ml Hayman's London Dry Gin

Premium tonic water

Lemon twist, to garnish

## Method

Add the ice and gin to a high ball glass.

Top up with premium tonic water.

Garnish with a lemon twist and serve.

# ENGLISH RUBY FIZZ

This pretty pink cocktail can be made with fresh raspberries.
(Serve it in a high ball glass).

Preparation time: 5 minutes | Serves 1

## Ingredients

50ml London Dry Gin

20ml lime juice

10ml sugar syrup or grenadine

4–8 fresh raspberries

Cubed ice

Ginger ale

Lime slice and fresh raspberries, to garnish

## Method

Combine the gin, lime juice, sugar syrup or grenadine and raspberries in a shaker and then shake well.

Strain the cocktail into a high ball glass with plenty of ice.

Top up with ginger ale.

Garnish with a lime wheel and raspberries.

# *Gin as it* SHOULD BE

The long-forgotten taste of vintage gin has been brought back
to life by Jensen's Gin in Bermondsey...

Jensen's Gin, which is produced by Bermondsey Gin Ltd., was created by Christian Jensen, a Danish-born Londoner with a passion for the lost art of vintage London gins. His journey into the world of gin began in 2000, when, after having lived in Bermondsey since 1987, he was transferred to Tokyo.

During his five years in Tokyo, Christian was intrigued by a delicious old gin that was served to him in a bar – the taste was nothing like the gin he was used to. He learnt that the differences in taste were due to the industrialisation of gin production from many small distilleries to a few huge ones. Christian's eyes were opened.

From joking with the bartender that he should make a 'proper' gin back in London, Christian actually came back to the UK and put this into practice. It was the early 2000s when Christian approached Thames Distillers and asked them to make him a gin like the ones he had been drinking in Tokyo. Between Christian and Charles Maxwell, a recipe was developed, and, after many hurdles, by 2004 the initial production of 100 cases (1200 bottles) of Jensen's Bermondsey Dry Gin were ready.

The bottles were gifted to friends, as well as sold in a shop at Borough Market, where the gin became extremely popular. A few years later, one of his new-found fans predicted that the gin market was about to undergo massive growth and suggested to Christian that an Old Tom would be a nice addition to the Jensen's Gin brand. After a period of research, Christian discovered a distiller's notebook that had an Old Tom recipe from 1840 – this was used to create Jensen's Old Tom Gin, which has been available since August 2008.

The production of these two gins at Thames Distillers continued for 8 years until 2012, when he decided that he needed to make the gin himself. He bought a still and began working with a chemist (to distill for him) and a bartender (who knew the drinks scene inside-out).

Today the business has expanded into a unique Anglo-Scandinavian team. This unusual heritage balances Scandi flavour composition and aesthetics with British craftsmanship and an appreciation of traditional botanicals. The British wheat spirit is distilled in small batches using traditional gin botanicals, creating a finely balanced gin that honours the long-lost London gin style.

Jensen's remind us that there's really nothing new about Jensen's Gin... and it is this simple fact that actually makes it different. Distilled in the heart of Bermondsey, Jensen's is 'gin as it was' – it is gin as it should be.

**JENSEN'S
LONDON DISTILLED
OLD TOM GIN**

Jensen's Old Tom is
made to a recipe found
in a distiller's notebook
from the 1800s. With
a bold, earthy flavour,
it can be used in place
of London Dry gin in
almost any gin cocktail
and makes an excellent
gin and tonic.

**jensen's**

When Christian Jensen
first tasted the vintage
gins from London's lost
distilleries, he began
a journey. Creating a
finely balanced gin that
honoured these forgotten
recipes became his
obsession. That's why
Jensen's is distilled in
small batches, using only
traditional gin botanicals.
So there's really nothing
new about Jensen's, and
that's why it's different.
Distilled in Bermondsey,
London, Jensen's is gin as
it was. Gin as it should be.

**LONDON DISTILLED
BERMONDSEY DRY GIN**

70CL 43% VOL.

# Jensen's Gin

## JENSEN'S GIN & TONIC

Our Bermondsey Dry's delicate balance between juniper and citrus notes compliment the cinchona in any good tonic.
For a Jensen's twist on the classic G&T, fill a glass with ice, add a generous measure of Jensen's Bermondsey Dry, charge with BTW – Bermondsey Tonic Water's historical tonic – and garnish with a sprig of rosemary.

Preparation time: 2 minutes | Serves 1

### Ingredients

Ice

1 measure Jensen's Bermondsey Dry

Bermondsey Tonic Water, to top up

Sprig of rosemary, to garnish

### Method

Fill a glass with ice.

Add a generous measure of Jensen's Bermondsey Dry.

Charge with BTW (Bermondsey Tonic Water's historic tonic).

Garnish with a sprig of rosemary.

# Jensen's Gin
# BERMONDSEY DRY WITH FENTIMEN'S ROSE LEMONADE

As an alternative to tonic, combine our Bermondsey Dry
with Fentimen's Rose Lemonade, lemon wheels and plenty of ice.
Fentimen's floral flavours work beautifully with our juniper
and citrus notes, creating a crisp and refreshing drink.

Preparation time: 2 minutes | Serves 1

## Ingredients

Ice

1 measure Jensen's Bermondsey Dry

Fentimen's Rose Lemonade, to top up

Lemon wheel, to garnish

## Method

Fill a glass with ice.

Add a generous measure of Jensen's Bermondsey Dry.

Top up with Fentimen's Rose Lemonade.

Garnish with a lemon wheel.

# *Living* HISTORY

In a city made of destination points, LASSCO bar & dining is undoubtedly one of its must-goes. In fact, must-go, must-see, and must-eat just about sums it up perfectly!

To walk through London is to walk through history. It comes with the territory when you're strolling one of the world's oldest and greatest cities. Nowhere is this more apparent than when you visit LASSCO's Bermondsey complex on Ropewalk. The framing and atmosphere is provided by a series of vast Victorian railway arches: symbols of the point where London became the world's great imperial centre, and flexed its muscles by remaking the city anew as a song of speed, connection, communication, and progress.

Set within these are LASSCO Ropewalk's main warehouse, Britain's first stop for architectural antiques, salvage, and curios. There's also a working timber yard where reclaimed timber is given a new lease of life; restaurants and cafés; and Maltby Street Market, which comes to life at the weekend. Managed by LASSCO, this started in 2010 as a small 6-stall produce-led market. However, it's grown over the years, and with outlets like St John's, Torzino and Little Bird Gin now permanent fixtures among the arches it's established itself as one of South London's most popular markets.

Of course, shopping and browsing simply aren't complete without a place to eat and rest your feet. Launched in 2017, and headed by Jerome Slesinski, LASSCO bar & dining has provided a similarly unique experience. Open seven days a week for breakfast and coffee and for lunch and dinner from midweek on, the emphasis is on serving seasonal, ingredient-led dishes, complemented by the drinks menu in an atmosphere that's relaxed and relaxing. The set-up takes advantage of a thriving local food and drink scene by reaching out into the Bermondsey area to showcase the best of what's on offer. Produce from the highly-regarded Neal's Yard, England Preserves, and Ice Cream Union, for example, and beer from local craft brewers, wine from local merchants, and London-roasted coffee round out a satisfying menu.

It's an area rich in history. To the east, Ropewalk's arches cross the Neckinger, which enters the Thames at Jacob's Island. Made famous as the lair of Oliver Twist's murderous Bill Sykes, it was once the site of one of London's earliest and worst slums. Cleared to make way for the railways and warehouses that still stand today, to walk through Ropewalk now, is to walk through part of London's rich history, and its ever-changing landscape. Incredible, evocative, and packed with things to see and do, and places to eat and drink, it is, as we said, a must-see!

LASSCO

LASSCO

THE OLD BERMONDSEY BREWERY

ST JOHN MALTBY

# LASSCO Bar & Dining
## ORCHARD SPRITZ

Perfect for sultry London summer nights, or lazy Sunday afternoon garden parties, LASSCO bar & dining offers the perfect drink for any occasion…

Preparation time: 5 minutes | Cooking time: 30 minutes | Serves 1

## Ingredients

### For the syrup:

50g honeysuckle flowers, dried (available from Asian supermarkets)

500ml water

1kg Demerara sugar

### For the drink (per glass):

15ml 'Our London' vodka

10ml honeysuckle syrup

100ml sparkling wine

45ml apple sorbet (we get ours from Ice Cream Union, who are local to us)

## Method

### To make the syrup

In a heavy-bottomed pan, place the water, the Demerara sugar and the honeysuckle flowers over a low heat and stir gently until boiled. Shutting off the heat, allow the mixture to cool and steep for 30 minutes before straining the syrup through a sieve.

### To make the spritz

Place all of the ingredients for the drink into a chilled martini or wine glass before topping with the sparkling wine of your choice, and garnishing with a honeysuckle flower.

Serve, drink and enjoy!

# Maltby Street Market

# VEGAN CARROT, WOOD EAR MUSHROOM, TOFU AND WATER CHESTNUT GYOZA

Down in South London, the Gyoza Guys put together their spin on a classic Japanese pan-fried dumpling recipe...

Preparation time: 5 minutes | Cooking time: 30 minutes | Serves 2-4

## Ingredients

1 onion

2 carrots

100g firm tofu

100g wood ear mushrooms, dried

1 inch ginger root

50g water chestnuts

10ml soy sauce (dark)

10ml mirin

10ml sesame oil

1g Japanese pepper

Vegan gyoza skins (1 packet)

2 tbsp vegetable oil

Cornflour, for dusting

### To serve:

Ponzu soy sauce or black vinegar (to taste)

## Method

Peel and finely dice the onion before then peeling and grating the carrots, the ginger, and the water chestnuts. Soak the wood ear mushrooms in warm water until soft, chop finely, and put to one side. Pressing the tofu to remove any excess liquid, crumble it with your fingers.

Placing a non-stick saucepan on a medium heat, add the oil. When hot, add the onions and cook gently until they caramelise to a deep brown colour. If they are cooking too quickly and are in danger of burning, turn the heat down. Then, add the grated carrot and continue cooking gently to remove the excess moisture. Once this is gone, add the grated ginger and continue to cook gently until all of the excess moisture is gone.

At this point, deglaze the pan by adding the soy sauce and heating until it has evaporated. Then, add the mirin and cook gently until it reduces by half. At this point, when the mix is slightly wet, add the wood ear mushrooms and half of the sesame oil and heat through.

Removing the pan from the heat, add the tofu and the Japanese pepper and combine well, adding salt to season and the last of the sesame oil. Adding three-quarters of a tablespoon of mixture to the middle of each dumpling skin, wet with a little water to pleat or close, and then place on a tray dusted with cornflour (to prevent sticking). Continue until all of the mixture has been parcelled up.

Heat a frying pan with a little oil, place the gyoza in the pan and fry on one side until golden brown before adding a little water and covering to steam to finish (approximately 3-5 minutes).

Serve while hot with ponzu soy sauce or black vinegar to taste.

# The PERFECT CURE

An award-winning local smokehouse in Crystal Palace, London Smoke & Cure is an exciting modern business that has artisan heritage at its heart.

London Smoke & Cure is a concept from Ross Mitchell, an ambitious foodie with a passion for innovation and a love of traditional craftsmanship. He launched his business when he got tired of spending too much time in front of a computer screen. "I yearned for an occupation where I could produce something unique and tangible, and through which feel more connected with my customers" says Ross.

In the early days, the smoking was done in a simple wooden box in the garden. Come rain or shine (and often armed with a torch in the dark!), Ross took a doggedly scientific approach to perfecting his salt and smoke blends. It was a rudimentary set-up, but one that was driven by passion and enthusiasm for quality, authenticity and integrity.

"Through that time I was refining the curing process" he says "to a point where I could capture a perfect moment of freshness in these superb quality ingredients. That's what separates us from others that can make products too salty, or with a smoke level that is unbalanced." By 2016 the well-equipped London Smoke & Cure smokehouse was completed, a unique and creative space that embodies the ancient traditions of this craft with the facilities to push the boundaries of what quality and flavour can mean for smoked produce.

Placing himself firmly at the heart of his community is vital for Ross. He uses sustainable local woods and insists on using ingredients that are ethical, of exceptional quality, and as local as possible. Now strongly integrated in the local economy, he thinks that being so closely linked to his customers is one of the things that keeps his business strong. Bumping into his customers in the park or pub keeps him connected to their needs. "The feedback I get from my customers is crucial, the products are theirs as much as they are mine so I really believe we're in it together."

As the only smokehouse south of the river he specialises in both cold and hot smoking, with a range that changes with the seasons. The cold-smoked selection includes dry-cured organic smoked streaky bacon, twice-smoked cheddar and an award winning smoked cashew nut butter. And from the hot-smoked range there's smoked duck and chicken, pastrami and pork belly amongst others. He is especially proud of his sashimi-grade cold smoked Scottish salmon, "it's like nothing else, so fresh and buttery."

Ross describes how things are going: "Everything we do is about using the highest form of craftsmanship to make small batches of produce that are exceptionally fresh and authentic. Production is growing fast and I love it that from our quiet little corner in Crystal Palace we're developing great relationships with customers right across the city. I can hardly wait to see how we grow next."

London Smoke & Cure

MOKE & CURE

HANDMADE DELI & STREETFOOD

# London Smoke & Cure
# SMOKED DUCK BREAST AND LENTIL WITH CHERRY

We love this recipe because it's elegant and yet so simple, and it really shines when using our premium smoked duck breast. It's a great meal which seems to eat well whatever the season or occasion.

Preparation time: 15 minutes | Cooking time: 25 minutes | Serves 4

## Ingredients

2 shallots, finely chopped

2 garlic cloves, finely chopped

120ml olive oil

200g Puy lentils, rinsed

500ml chicken stock

1 lime, zested and juiced

40g parsley, finely chopped

40g runner beans

2 London Smoke & Cure smoked duck breasts

100g fresh cherries, pitted and halved

20g baby kale

Salt and cracked black pepper

## Method

Sweat the shallots and garlic in a pan with a good glug of the olive oil. Add the lentils and cover with plenty of chicken stock. Bring to the boil and simmer for 15-20 minutes, until cooked but retaining a bite.

Drain well, transfer to a mixing bowl and, whilst hot, add the lime zest and juice with a few tablespoons of the olive oil, along with a good pinch of salt and cracked pepper. Set aside to cool. Once cool, mix in the chopped parsley.

Blanch the runner beans, drain and set side.

In a hot frying pan add 2 tablespoons of olive oil and crisp the smoked duck breast until dark golden brown and rest on a plate. In the same frying pan cook the cherries until softened.

To plate, start with a generous spoon of the lentils and add the beans. Thinly slice the duck and add to the plate. Spoon over the cherries, add some of the cooking juices, garnish with the baby kale and serve.

# London Smoke & Cure
## SMOKED CASHEW BUTTER ICE CREAM

This is the purest form of ice cream and the joy of it is that you don't need an
ice cream maker, nor do you need to churn it in any shape or form.
Just make, freeze and then devour!

Preparation time: 10 minutes | Freeze time: 2-3 hours | Serves 4

## Ingredients

*3 tbsp organic maple syrup*

*2 tbsp London Smoke & Cure
smoked cashew nut butter*

*3 egg yolks*

*250ml single or double cream*

## Method

Heat the maple syrup in a saucepan till just warmed. Place the cashew butter and egg yolks
in a medium bowl. Whisk in the warm maple syrup and then whip in the cream. Pour into
a freezer-proof dish, then freeze for 2-3 hours or until firm.

Take out of the freezer 5-10 minutes before serving alongside a warm brownie or with
warm chocolate and maple sauce sauce.

# *The famous fish* EXPERIENCE

Celebrating 30 years of being one of South London's (and the country's) top chippies, Olley's Fish Experience has become synonymous with the very best of sustainable fish.

Situated across from Brockwell Park, Olley's has been an essential part of the Herne Hill community since it opened in 1987. From a small takeaway, owner Harry had ambitions to expand his much-loved little shop into something a little different to any other fish and chip shop.

"It was clear from the start that people would like somewhere to eat in," Harry explains, looking back to the early days. "So, I put a table and four chairs in the corner – and would tell people to take a seat at 'table 2'." This intriguing number had the desired effect and became a talking point in the shop, as people would ask him, "but where is table 1?". Harry knew that one day, it would be one of many tables.

His aspiration to expand the shop into a restaurant became a reality 12 years later, when the unit next door became available. Since then, the restaurant has been packed full of customers, so Harry dreams of expanding even further to create more space inside.

The quality of the fish has seen Olley's win numerous awards, including being listed in the top 60 fish and chip shops by the Seafish Authority – the Oscar's of the fish and chip world!

Harry is passionate about sustainability, but for him, this isn't a word to be thrown around lightly. He cooks fish that is only sustainable and MSC-credited, often being local fish from British waters, but sometimes his search takes him far and wide for the finest-quality certified fish and shellfish, such as his king prawns, which come from Australia and are the best-tasting prawns he has ever tried.

Alongside the most popular options of cod, haddock and hake, Harry loves to offer things that are not on your usual chippy menu. Think grilled herring, mussels, lemon sole or redfish, which Olley's is proudly the first place to have MSC-credited in the whole country.

Another thing that has set Olley's apart from the crowd is their enviable gluten-free options. What started with gluten-free Tuesdays has become so popular that gluten-free fish and chips are now available every day, alongside the usual fish and chips.

With a huge fan base across South London, it is no surprise that Olley's are a popular choice for party orders – whether it's a wedding for 100 or a party around the corner, Olley's are taking their award-winning fish and chips further afield than their Herne Hill home.

# Olley's Fish Experience
# GRILLED SALMON & SALAD

Use fresh and delicate salmon fillets for this dish, which is equally delicious served hot or cold.

Preparation time: 20 minutes | Cooking time: 8 minutes | Serves 2

## Ingredients

**For the salad:**

½ yellow pepper, deseeded and diced

½ red pepper, deseeded and diced

½ orange pepper, deseeded and diced

50g coriander, chopped

50g flat leaf parsley, chopped

100g mixed leaf lettuce

50g beetroot, grated

Sea salt and freshly ground pepper

**For the salmon:**

2 tbsp lemon or lime juice

6 tbsp good-quality olive oil

2 x 200g salmon fillets

Sea salt and freshly ground pepper

## Method

**For the salad**

Mix all the ingredients in a large bowl, adding seasoning to taste. Keep chilled and give it another mix before serving.

**For the salmon**

Mix together the lemon or lime juice, olive oil and seasoning, and massage onto the salmon. If you're going to cook the fish with the skin on and would like a crisper skin, only add sea salt directly on the skin. Otherwise add salt to taste when eating.

Heat the grill to medium. Grill the fish for 4 minutes on each side (skin facing the heat first), then turn over until cooked through. Only turn the fish once to keep the fish from breaking up. Serve hot or cold with the salad. Enjoy.

# Where spooning leads
# TO FORKING

A nod to the London 'caff' on one hand, while joyfully immersed in the farm landscape, Piccalilli Caff is a fun and friendly eatery based at Surrey Docks Farm.

Brixton-born Scarlett was lucky enough to grow up in South London, where myriad cuisines from around the world are on offer every day. A food-lover of course, but she is also passionate about people, and dreamed of starting her own business in the hospitality sector – something where she could look after people, chat to them and indulge her love of food and farming.

She jumped at the opportunity to take on the resident café at Surrey Docks Farm. The magical spot situated right on the Thames path and within the 2-acre farm enchanted Scarlett from the outset. It's a unique location in that you are surrounded by farm animals yet with a view of Canary Wharf – there aren't many places with such a setting!

Being in the capital, Scarlett's playful take on a London greasy spoon is a fun nod to its wider setting. However, the simply plated breakfasts and brunches are freshly cooked, locally sourced and 100% homemade. The 'build your own' breakfast is the star of the morning menu – people can create their own breakfast plate, just paying for the items they want. No more uneaten tomatoes going to waste! From homemade beans on toast to the full works, take your pick. This approach has firstly cut down on food waste enormously, but also provided accessible, flexible options for guests.

The open kitchen allows the chefs to chat to diners – often about their twin passions of food and gardening. "We have an allotment in Bow on the canal, where chef Pete grows an abundance of interesting and unusual things I'd never seen before, like nasturtium root and cucamelons," explains Scarlett.

The farm setting acts as a nice reminder of where the food comes from, as well as celebrating seasonality, which is really important to Scarlett: "You can step on to the farm and see how it is grown, and then come inside and have it cooked to its best, all in one lovely, affordable day out."

This magical spot on a working farm on the banks of the river Thames is the perfect place to showcase London-inspired food. In fact, with the historic 'ting ting ting' sound of Kevin Boys Blacksmith in the background, there is no mistaking this captivating corner of the capital.

# Piccalilli Caff
# AUBERGINE EGGS IN PURGATORY

Warming spices, fresh herbs and perfectly cooked eggs come together in this delicious dish. Top it with crumbled feta, chopped parsley and a sprinkling of freshly chopped chilli for the perfect finish.

Preparation time: 15 minutes | Cooking time: 30 minutes | Serves 6

## Ingredients

3 red onions, diced

2 garlic cloves, finely chopped

2 aubergines, diced

1 tsp fennel seeds

1 tsp nigella seeds

1 tsp coriander seeds

1 tsp cumin seeds

Few juniper berries

1 bay leaf

Few thyme sprigs

1 tsp smoked paprika

1 tsp Hungarian paprika

Large dash of red wine

2 tins of tomatoes

Olive oil, for cooking

Feta, crumbled, for topping

Parsley, chopped, to garnish

Chilli, chopped, to garnish

## Method

Preheat the oven to 200°c. Add the diced onions to a pan with a little olive oil, and cook out until softened. Add the garlic and aubergines.

In a dry frying pan, toast all the seeds, then add them to the onion and aubergine mixture. Add the herbs, juniper berries and both types of paprika, then add the red wine and tomatoes and bring to a simmer. Cook out until the aubergines are soft.

Place the cooked aubergine mixture into a frying pan, crack 6 eggs into the pan and bake in the preheated oven until the eggs are set. Top with crumbled feta cheese, chopped parsley and a sprinkle of fresh chilli. Enjoy!

# Piccalilli Caff
## SCOTCH EGG

The Piccalilli Scotch eggs are made with a flavoursome sausage meat mix and
coated in crispy panko breadcrumbs.

Preparation time: 30 minutes | Cooking time: 20 minutes | Serves 4

## Ingredients

1 tsp fennel seeds

800g pork sausage meat

1 white onion, finely chopped

2 large carrots, grated

¼ tsp allspice

Dash of Worcestershire sauce

3 juniper berries, crushed

Pinch of smoked paprika

6 hen's eggs

Flour, for rolling

Panko breadcrumbs, for coating

Salt and pepper

## Method

Toast the fennel seeds in a dry frying pan on the hob until they smell fragrant, but do
not let them go brown. Mix them with the raw sausage meat, the chopped onion, grated
carrots, allspice, Worcestershire sauce, crushed juniper berries, a pinch of paprika and a
pinch each of salt and pepper.

Split the mixture into four equal portions.

Boil four of the hen's eggs for 6 minutes, then remove them from the water and peel the
shells off them under cold, running water.

Roll one portion of the sausage mix into a ball and squash it on the palm of your hand.
Roll one peeled egg in flour, then place the egg in the sausage meat and squeeze it gently
around the egg to cover. Repeat with the other three eggs and sausage meat portions. You
will then have four tennis ball-sized meat-covered eggs. Roll these again in flour.

Crack the two remaining eggs into a dish and whisk with a fork. Put the panko breadcrumbs
in a flat dish with sides. Dip the balls in the egg and roll in the panko crumbs until evenly
covered. Heat the oil for deep-frying to 130°c. Deep-fry the Scotch eggs for 13 minutes
or until golden and the sausage meat is cooked.

# Piccalilli Caff
# MOROCCAN ORANGE CAKE

This aromatic drizzle cake is bursting with flavour from citrus, cloves, vanilla and cinnamon. Decorated with pistachios and edible rose petals, it is a delight to the eye as well as the palate.

Preparation time: 30 minutes | Cooking time: 45 minutes | Serves 8

## Ingredients

**For the cake:**

300ml sunflower oil

250g caster sugar

5 eggs

50g self-raising flour

300g ground almonds

1 tbsp baking powder

2 tbsp agave syrup

**For the topping:**

1 orange, zest and juice

½ lemon, zest and juice

2 small cinnamon sticks

½ vanilla pod

2 cloves

4 tbsp agave syrup

**To decorate:**

Toasted pistachios

Edible rose petals

## Method

**For the cake**

Preheat the oven to 180°c. Grease and line a loaf tin. Whisk together the oil and sugar in a mixing bowl. Add the eggs, one by one, then add the flour, ground almonds and baking powder and mix to combine. Finally, add the agave syrup and mix again. Pour the mixture into a loaf tin and bake in the preheated oven for 40-45 minutes until a skewer, inserted into the centre, comes out clean.

**For the topping**

Put all the topping ingredients in a pan and reduce the mixture by half. Use a skewer or cocktail stick to make holes all over the top of the cake, then pour the syrup over the cake while it is still hot.

**To decorate**

Decorate with small handful of toasted pistachios and rose petals.

# *Perfectly* PRESERVED

Bringing the best of cured, pickled and preserved foods to South London, Salt + Pickle is a unique eatery in Crystal Palace.

When it opened in June 2017, Salt + Pickle brought a new and innovative concept to the gastronomic scene of Crystal Palace – taking the best-quality ingredients from local suppliers and preserving them using ancient techniques.

Head chef Henry Freestone takes the lead role in devising the menu, which showcases the seasons throughout the year. "We work with our suppliers to find out what is at its best at the time, and we create our menus to make the most out of these ingredients", says Henry.

When it comes to curing, they always go for the finest ingredients possible. They cure their own sashimi-grade salmon in the restaurant, as well as beef fillet from Lincolnshire Red cattle – the oldest cattle breed in the UK. They are known for their potted shrimp and smoked duck breast, as well as their many homemade pickles. They have also started delving into the nutritious world of fermented foods, with homemade sauerkraut now on the menu.

Being located just up the road from their sister business Good Taste, Salt + Pickle have easy access to some of the finest artisan cheeses, charcuterie, beers and wines in the capital. The wine list is impressively long, featuring more unusual offerings that people may not have tried before. They also offer wine flights that allow diners to try a few over the course of their meal.

23-year-old Henry brings an adventurous approach to the kitchen, having already accrued 8 years of experience. With so much preparation having to be done in advance – as is the intrinsic nature of preserved foods – it allows him to fit the cooking in and around his other passion of music. Henry boasts the title World Reggae Champion 2015 – showing that his creativity, energy and love of art shines through in every aspect of his life, not just the kitchen.

# Salt+Pickle
# DILL PICKLES

This simple recipe is best after about 1 week in a sterilised jar.

Preparation time: 10 minutes, plus 1 week to pickle | Cooking time: 10 minutes | Makes 1 large jar

## Ingredients

2 cucumbers

300ml cider vinegar

200g caster sugar, or to taste

1 large pinch of salt

1 tsp turmeric

1 tbsp yellow mustard seeds

1 red chilli, finely sliced

2 bay leaves

¼ bunch of dill

## Method

Slice the cucumbers into 4mm slices and set aside.

In a pan, heat the vinegar with the sugar, salt, turmeric, mustard seeds and chilli.

Meanwhile, place the bay leaves in a sterilised jar with the dill. Push all the cucumber slices on top of the bay and dill in the jar.

Once the vinegar mixture has come to the boil, taste it and check to see if it is sweet enough. Add more sugar if needed. Pour the hot vinegar into the jar until full, then seal the lid. This will be ready in 1 week.

# Salt+Pickle
# APPLE & PEAR CHUTNEY

Warm spices complement apples and pears in this tasty chutney. It will be ready after about a week, but the longer you leave it, the better.

Preparation time: 20 minutes | Cooking time: 1 hour | Makes 2-3 jars

## Ingredients

6 apples

6 pears

1 stick of cinnamon

1 tsp ground ginger

100g soft brown sugar

150ml white wine vinegar

1 large pinch of salt

## Method

Peel, core and cut the apples and pears into 2cm cubes. Place them into a large pan and add all of the remaining ingredients.

Heat to slowly cook out the vinegar, being careful that it doesn't catch. Once the vinegar has cooked out and the fruit is semi-puréed and shiny, remove the pan from the heat.

Decant the mixture into sterilised jars. This will be ready in about a week, but the longer you leave it, the better.

# The Good LIFE!

Nicola Simons and Single Variety Co are taking a refreshingly direct approach to classic jams and preserves to stunning effect...

We tend to think of jams and preserves in a country context: fields of raspberry or gooseberry bushes waiting to be stripped, maybe; or jam-pans on the stoves in country kitchens. But if the countryside is where the good stuff is grown, Merton Abbey Mills' Single Variety Co is proving that South London is most definitely where the good stuff is made!

Like all the best ideas, founder Nicola's was a simple one. To make the best jams and preserves, start by finding the very best varieties of fruit, and then only use that single variety in any one batch. To this end, Single Variety Co sources fruit direct from small local UK farmers and only ever takes fruit in season. Then its recipes are made using a higher fruit content and lower sugar content than traditional jams and preserves; and only ever in small batches to preserve as much of the fruit's flavours as possible.

Take the Maravilla Raspberry Preserve, for example, which uses nothing but raspberries, sugar, and lemon juice to generate its deliciously tart and fruity flavour. The proof of the spreading is in the eating, of course, but it's an approach that's left more than just customers coming back for more. Single Variety Co's Seville Orange Marmalade recently won Gold in the 2017 World Marmalade Awards, making it one of the best marmalades in the world as voted by experts – which is some accolade!

This growing reputation has seen Single Variety Co taken on in some of the UK's best outlets, including Harvey Nichols flagship Knightsbridge store, and firmly establish itself in some of the UK's best foodie markets. Oh, and they sell direct via their website, so there's no excuse not to try the good stuff that's on offer.

And why not? The classics are all present and correct – scrumptious strawberry jams and marvellous marmalades – but there are some wonderful twists. The Jalapeño Jam which combines fresh British jalapeños with cider vinegar is a perfect meat or cheeseboard condiment, for example, while the Anaheim Chilli Jam balances warmth and sweetness to make a perfect marinade for prawns and chicken.

When it comes to food, as in all things in life, the devil is in the detail. So, next time you're reaching for something to spread on your daily bread or to make your cheeseboard pop with flavour, make sure it's something Single Variety Co have made – they really are that good!

# Single Variety Co
# BLACKBERRY PRESERVE

At Single Variety Co we love our Blackberry Preserve. We like to use Loch Ness blackberries, which are bigger and juicier than the average blackberry and create a deliciously chunky preserve. These can be found in all good British hedgerows in August and September ... so get picking!

Preparation time: 1 hour | Makes 6-8 220g jars

## Ingredients

*1kg blackberries*

*900g jam sugar (jam sugar contains the added pectin needed for this recipe)*

*30g fresh lemon juice*

## Method

Start by sterilising your jars by washing them thoroughly before placing in a warm oven at 160°c for 15 minutes. Old jars can be re-used provided they are cleaned thoroughly first, but remember to always use new screw-on lids.

Then, put the berries and lemon juice into a large stainless steel pan – a Maslin pan is best as they are designed for preserving. Cook these over a low heat for around 15 minutes until they are soft and plenty of juice has been released. Once this has happened, add the sugar, keeping the pan on a low heat for a further 10 minutes, or until the sugar has dissolved. Stir occasionally to prevent the mixture sticking to the bottom of the pan.

Once the sugar has dissolved, increase the heat to maximum and bring to a rapid rolling boil. Boil until setting point is reached, approximately 10 minutes. The best way to tell the setting point is to use a plate that has been kept in the freezer. Drop a small amount of jam onto the cold plate, and then return it to the fridge for 5 minutes. Take the pan off the heat to prevent it cooking more. After 5 minutes, push your finger through the jam. If it wrinkles then it's ready, and the preserve in the pan can be poured into the jars.

Do this using a funnel, filling each jar to 2mm from the top of the jar before screwing the lid on. Once sealed, the preserve will keep for up to a year. Once opened, though, keep it in the fridge!

### To serve

We'd recommend a blackberry sponge pudding – see the next recipe!

# Single Variety Co
# BLACKBERRY SPONGE PUDDING

Our favourite winter pudding is a sponge pudding topped with one of our delicious jams. Although any kind of jam works, it's a great way to use the blackberry preserve from the previous recipe.

Preparation time: 15 minutes | Cooking time: 90 minutes | Serves 4

## Ingredients

4 tbsp blackberry preserve (or jam of your choice)

175g butter, softened

3 eggs

175g caster sugar

175g self-raising flour

1 tbsp milk

1 tsp vanilla extract

## Method

Grease a 1.2 litre pudding basin and place the blackberry preserve in the base.

Boil a kettle of water, put an upturned plate into a large saucepan, and add the boiling water up to the top of the plate. This creates a steamer – alternatively, use a steamer!

In a mixing bowl, cream together the butter and sugar and then beat in the eggs.

Gently fold in the flour until thoroughly mixed, then add the milk and vanilla extract and store until all of the ingredients have been thoroughly combined.

Spread this mixture on top of the blackberry preserve before covering the pudding basin with baking parchment and foil and securing it with string.

Stand the pudding on the upturned bowl in your saucepan and bring the pan or steamer to a gentle simmer.

Cover the pan with a tight-fitting lid and allow to steam for 1½ hours. Remember to check and top up the water occasionally to make sure that the pan doesn't boil dry.

To check that the pudding is done, insert a skewer through the foil and parchment lid through the centre of the pudding. If the skewer comes out clean – then the pudding is cooked. If some wet mixture comes out, then return to the steamer for a further 15-20 minutes before checking again.

Once cooked, uncover and turn the pudding onto a plate before serving straight away – preferably (for us!) with custard!

# Full of FLAVOUR

Strong, bold, vibrant... the foodie culture of Tooting is a celebration of international flavours and authentic dishes. Tuck in!

Tooting is a diverse, colourful and energetic community, and the eclectic culinary culture reflects this in a joyful medley of gastronomic offerings that delight all the senses. The Tooting Town Centre 'Full of Flavour' brand was developed to showcase this incredible foodie community and to celebrate Tooting as one of London's liveliest dining destinations.

Tooting Full of Flavour celebrates the authenticity of its dining scene, describing it as 'the real deal' – sometimes a bit chaotic, but always energetic and full of life! The diversity of this multicultural urban area is reflected in its rich food scene, which makes it one of the most exciting places to eat in the city.

In Tooting, you get a taste of the world from a local, neighbourhood atmosphere – from restaurants cooking up cuisines from around the globe to retailers selling everything from fresh fruit and vegetables to exotic spices, not to mention the lively street food scene.

The smells, sights and sounds can transport you around the world. The 'curry corridor' offers an array of delicacies, such as crispy dosas (potato-filled rice pancakes), barbecued sizzling meat, steaming hot naans, biryanis, vegetarian delights, Indian savoury snacks and colourful sweets, as made in the subcontinent. In an instant, you can move to authentic, mouth-watering Spanish fare, such as succulent prawns sautéed with garlic and chilli, crisp salt cod fritters or other tasty tapas favourites. Around the corner, you will be won over by Lebanese delights, such as falafel, mixed grills or baba ghanoush (grilled puréed aubergine mixed with sesame paste and lemon juice). And for those who are looking for a traditional English dish, there is classic pie, mash, mushy peas and liquor on offer. Quirky drinking establishments and eateries can be found in the indoor markets. Head to Tooting Market, for example, for great wines, gins and craft beers, as well as places to sit down while you eat and people-watch to your heart's content.

Back on the streets of Tooting, gastro pubs and trendy cocktail bars provide broad options for drinking, while cafés serve up brunches and meals to suit all tastes. With so many choices for the hungry visitor and local, Tooting is certainly living up to its 'Full of Flavour' description!

# *The holy* TRINITY

Since setting his flag firmly in South London's fertile territory Adam Byatt's Trinity restaurant, Upstairs at Trinity, and Union-Bistro have gone from strength to strength...

Launched in 2006, Adam Byatt's Trinity Restaurant has seen over a decade of the capital's food fads and competitors come and go by focusing on the things that are important. A destination for food lovers since it opened, Trinity has become renowned for its sophisticated, modern interpretations of classic dishes. Whilst keeping the heart and soul that have made them classics in the first place, Adam and his team bring their menu into the contemporary moment with verve and élan. This isn't just us talking, though. Trinity's penchant for creative culinary interpretation has been critically recognized in the form of one of Michelin's coveted stars, recently awarded; while their exceptional attention to detail and consistency have won them an equally excellent word-of-mouth reputation. The emphasis is on taking the inspiration offered by the very best of what's available seasonally, turning it into a memorable gastronomic experience, and serving it up in Trinity's elegant privately-owned setting.

Upstairs at Trinity (the clue to the location being in the title!) came about to offer the discerning diner casual dining in its finest form. The self-contained dining space serves guests a perfectly-balanced selection of small plates from an ever-changing daily menu; all of which are cooked to order from an open island kitchen; and all of which are designed to share. It's a flexible innovative space too, available for reservations and exclusive hires as well as running special events and evenings that focus on everything from expert-led wine masterclasses to celebrated guest chef menus to simply a place to host a convivial Sunday lunch with those nearest and dearest to you. It offers its guests the chance to get closer to the cooking experience and to experience the passion and focus of the team in a fully immersive experience.

Whether the expansive, meticulous artistry of Trinity, or the intimacy of Upstairs at Trinity, both venues are driven by the attention to detail, consistency, and flair that have landed Adam Byatt and his team numerous awards and accolades, as well as a firm reputation for being one of the very best places to eat in not just South London, but the UK itself. Make a reservation, and get yourself down there. This is food that is not to be missed!

# Trinity Restaurant
# BUTTER POACHED NATIVE LOBSTER

It may seem like there are a lot of different elements to bring together with this sumptuous dish, but each stage is relatively simple – and it all comes together into something truly spectacular and worth your time!

Preparation time: 30 minutes | Cooking time: 2 hours 30 minutes | Serves 8

## Ingredients

2 x Cornish Blue lobster

**For the cocoa beans:**

300g podded cocoa beans

Mirepoix of vegetables (carrot, onion, celery, leek – cut large)

Small handful of fresh tarragon

100ml vegetable stock

**For the pickled girolles:**

200g prepped girolles

1 tsp mustard seeds

**For the sweet pickle:**

150g white sugar

150ml white wine vinegar

150ml water

**For the lobster butter:**

1 lobster head

200g unsalted butter

Spices (coriander seed, start anise, fennel seed)

Lemon zest

**For the lemon purée:**

10 Amalfi lemons

½ vanilla pod

100g caster sugar (plus extra for the blanching water)

50ml extra virgin olive oil

50ml lemon oil

Sea salt

**For the bisque:**

1 lobster head

50ml olive oil

1 star anise

½ tsp coriander seeds

½ tsp fennel seeds

4 black peppercorns

½ scraped vanilla pod (not seeds)

1 tomato, halved

200ml Armagnac

200ml white wine

1 litre fish stock

500ml water

Small cut of mirepoix vegetables

Viola flowers

Nasturtium flowers

## Method

Humanely prepare the lobsters by inserting a knife into the 'X' mark on its head. This will kill the lobster immediately. Twist and pull the head to remove it and reserve it for the Bisque and the Butter. Remove the claws from the head section. Tie the two tails together 'head to tail' so that they do not bend during the cooking.

Bring a pan of water to the boil that has been salted with 3% of its weight in salt, along with a handful of mirepoix vegetables and gently poach the tail for around 3 minutes, depending on its size, and the claws for around 5 minutes, again depending on size. This timing would work for a 500g lobster. Try to scale up approximately 1 minute for every 250g thereafter.

Chill the tail immediately in ice before peeling. The claws and knuckles are easier to crack when warm, so allow them to cool for 2 minutes so you can handle them before attempting this. Chill these immediately on a tray over ice.

To make the lobster bisque, first chop the head and gently sweat in olive oil. Add the spices, vanilla and the mirepoix and cook for 5 minutes or so to soften the vegetables. Add the Armagnac and flambé. Add the wine and heat until it has reduced by half. Add the fish stock and the water, along with the tomato then bring the whole to the boil and allow to simmer uncovered for 45 minutes.

After that, pass this mixture through a Mouli to crush the shells and extract all of the liquid before placing back on the heat and reducing to just before a glaze. Add a capful or two of the double cream, adjust with lemon juice to taste if necessary and use this to warm through the cocoa beans. Finish with fresh chopped tarragon.

To make the sweet pickle, place all of the ingredients into a pan, and then bring them to the boil before allowing it to cool.

To make the lightly pickled girolles, lightly toast the mustard seeds and cover with the pickle before bringing to the boil and then pour over the girolles before covering and allowing to cool.

To make the lemon purée, peel the zest off all of the lemons with a fine peeler. Blanch the zest for 2 minutes in boiling water lightly seasoned with salt and sweetened with 25% sugar. Do this 5 times in different changes of water, refreshing in ice water each time. On the final blanch, do not refresh in ice water but strain and transfer into a blender.

Blend with the sugar, vanilla, olive and lemon oils, a pinch of sea salt, the juice of half of the lemons and enough of the final blanching water to allow it to blend. The purée should be a perfect balance of sweet, tangy, and savoury.

To make the lobster butter, blend the whole head with the butter and the spices. Place in a vacuum pack bag and cook on steam at 80°c for 2 hours. Failing that, the butter can be cooked in a bowl set over a pan of simmering water. Pass through a double layer of muslin cloth and chill before serving.

### To serve

Place the lemon purée on the base of a hot, large flat plate. Add the cocoa beans mixed with the girolles to the centre of the plate, then add the poached lobster, the flowers and finish with the lobster stock and a drizzle of remaining butter.

# Watching the WATCHERS

Tucked away at the end of Bermondsey Street, this historic shelter for nineteenth-century guards is now brewing up a storm on one of London's foodiest streets.

It is difficult to imagine how anyone fits into the oddly-shaped building that is home to The Watch House. Nestled at the end of Bermondsey Street, it's almost magical how endless customers pile into the seemingly finite space like a masterful optical illusion unfolding on your morning commute. The site is, in fact, only 25 square meters but every inch has been designed to capitalise on this space and the historical features that make it so unique.

Although the site itself certainly makes The Watch House distinctive, it isn't the only thing that makes this quirky coffee shop a South London favourite. Their coffee is produced exclusively for them by boutique roasters so no one else has quite the same blend. The Watch House serves up a full, fruity roast perfectly complemented by Estate Dairy's organic milk and a selection of in-house baked goods that could tempt even the strongest will into saying 'oh, go on then.' Whether you're a hard-core espresso lover or someone seduced by silky lattes, this is third-wave coffee and accompaniments as they should be.

Quality is the gold standard watchword for The Watch House. It doesn't just apply to the coffee. Pop in around 12:30 and you will find the counters adorned with lush towers of thick cut sourdough sandwiches, ciabattas with marinated chicken, tuna melts and daily quiches, as well as soups all made from scratch in their central kitchen. This may be a young company but its ambition to be successful is apparent everywhere you look.

For those seeking something a little more mid-morning, they offer a varied brunch at their larger sister site at Tower Bridge. If you've had enough of poached eggs on avocado toast – and it is 'if' as they taste fantastic – try their Eggs in Purgatory: rich and creamy with a little kick from the chili and tomato sauce. A perfect way to start the day.

Both venues reach into their respective communities. Their walls are decorated with the work of local artists, for example, and are all available to purchase with the company taking no commission so the artist gets the full benefit.

With a third location on Fetter Lane in development, and two well-regarded venues already going great guns, The Watch House shows its firm, continued commitment to creating beautiful spaces, filling them with friendly people, and then filling those friendly people with great coffee, great food, and a great experience. People are voting with their feet – and that's always a good sign!

The Watch House

# The Watch House
# EGGS BENEDICT

This is our take on an established breakfast classic that can also double up as a hearty brunch or a light weekend lunch. There's a little prep involved but it's more than worth it, so get cooking...

Preparation time: 24 hours | Cooking time: 2 hours | Serves 2-4

## Ingredients

**For the honey-roast pulled ham:**

2½kg gammon joint, unsmoked

50g Demerara sugar

125g orange marmalade

100g honey

50g English mustard powder

250ml lemon juice

500ml apple cider

**For the hollandaise:**

1 egg yolk

½ tsp white wine vinegar

1 tsp lemon juice

225g butter

Salt, pinch

Black pepper, pinch

**For the poached eggs:**

2 eggs, large (we use St. Ewes)

½ tsp white wine vinegar

**To serve:**

Sourdough bread, sliced

Micro-parsley, handful

## Method

### To cook the honey roast ham

Begin by steeping the gammon overnight in a pot of water to remove excess salt. Then, prepare the marinade for the joint by mixing the Demerara sugar, orange marmalade, honey and English mustard into a thick paste and set aside.

After 24 hours, drain the pot and refilling it with fresh water. Bring this to the boil, before reducing it to a simmer for 2 hours. After 2 hours, drain the ham and remove the skin (making sure to leave a layer of fat on it for roasting) and then place it in a baking tray. Preheating the oven to 190°c, slather the ham in marinade and place in the oven. After 30 minutes, pour in the cider and lemon juice and cover the baking tray tightly with two layers of tin foil. Then, reduce the oven temperature to 150°c and allow the meat to slow cook for 3 hours. Remove from the ham from the oven, set it aside, and allow it to cool until you can pull it apart with your fingers.

### For the hollandaise sauce

Start by slowly melting the butter in a small saucepan over a low to medium heat. Once melted, skim the white solids from the melted butter. Bringing a half pan of water to the boil, separate the egg and add the yolk to a heat-resistant bowl that fits the top of the pan. Vigorously whisk the egg yolk over boiling water until it starts to become frothy and pale yellow in colour before adding in the clarified butter a little at a time as the mixture begins to emulsify and thicken, whisking continuously. During this process, it is important to not keep the bowl over the boiling water consistently so as to prevent the mixture from scrambling. Take the bowl off the heat every 30 seconds or so or while adding more butter. Continue until all butter has been used.

### Poaching the eggs

As you approach serving time, turn your attention to the poached eggs. Bringing a pan of water to the boil, add the white wine vinegar before reducing the heat to a simmer. Crack the eggs into a ramekin each and then, stirring a gentle whirlpool into the pan, add the eggs, allowing the white to wrap around the yolk. Gently tip the egg whites into the water first and then leave them to cook for exactly 3 minutes. Take a slotted spoon and remove the eggs from the water, cutting off any lose egg whites.

Place the poached eggs onto kitchen paper to remove excess water and dab dry.

### To serve

Take a loaf of your preferred bread (ours is sourdough), and cut a slice with the thickness of an inch or so. Grab a griddle pan and place it on a medium/high heat and drizzle a little olive oil onto the bread and place it on the pan for a few minutes until crisp.

Place the thick slice of sourdough onto a plate and then start to assemble the dish. Add 200g of the gammon to the sourdough following up with the poached eggs, 2 tablespoons of hollandaise sauce and garnish with micro parsley. Season with salt and freshly ground black pepper.

# The Watch House

# SLOW-COOKED HARISSA CHICKEN FLATBREAD WITH HOMEMADE ALIOLI AND FRESH CORIANDER

Although this takes a little preparation, the result is a flavoursome dish perfect for snacks or main meals with friends and family.

Preparation time: 24 hours | Cooking time: 7-8 hours | Serves 6

## Ingredients

**For the slow-cooked harissa chicken:**

4 chicken breasts

5 tbsp harissa paste

5 tbsp Greek yoghurt, natural

2 pinches salt & pepper

3 tsp paprika

**For the homemade alioli (makes 350ml):**

2 large egg yolks

300ml olive oil

2 garlic cloves, peeled and minced

1 tsp salt

1 tbsp lemon juice

**To serve:**

4 panuozzi, or flatbread

1 handful coriander leaves

## Method

### For the slow-cooked harissa chicken

Start by mixing together the harissa, paprika and yoghurt in a large bowl before seasoning well with salt and pepper. Then, place the chicken breasts in the bowl and turn them to make sure that they are fully covered in the marinade. Place in the fridge and leave for a minimum of 2 hours, but preferably 24 to allow the flavours to penetrate the meat. The longer you leave them, the better the dish will taste!

To cook, place the chicken breasts in a slow cooker. Make sure that they aren't overlapping, and then cover and cook on a low heat for 7-8 hours. Turn halfway through.

### For the alioli

Separate out the egg yolks from the egg whites. Discard the whites (or use them in another recipe) and then set the yolks aside. Peel and mince the garlic before adding it to the egg yolks. Add the salt and then whisk vigorously. Once the mixture is thoroughly combined, start adding small amounts of olive oil to it, whisking continually until it starts to thicken. Once it starts to thicken add the remaining olive oil in a steady stream, whisking all the while until it reaches the consistency of mayonnaise. At this point, add the lemon juice and mix it in. Season with salt and pepper to taste.

### To serve

Taking the chicken out of the slow cooker, pull or cut it into thick strips. Spread a generous tablespoon of alioli onto your flatbread, add the pulled chicken and a handful of fresh coriander leaves and tuck in!

# The DIRECTORY

These great businesses have supported the making of this book; please support and enjoy them.

**Aga's Little Deli**
49 Dartmouth road
Forest Hill
London SE23 3HN
Telephone: 07880 760915
*We love real food. Quality over quantity.*

**The Alma**
95 Church Road
Crystal Palace
London SE19 2TA
Telephone: 0208 768 1885
Website: www.thealmapub.com
*Relaxed and friendly pub with a great reputation for quality ales, wines and great British pub food.*

**Art & Craft**
2A Streatham High Road
Streatham Hill
London SW16 1DB
Website: www.artandcraft.london
*Art on the walls, craft beer on the shelves.*

**Art & Craft**
52 Knights Hill
West Norwood
London SW27 0JD
Website: www.artandcraft.london
*Art on the walls, craft beer on the shelves.*

**Art & Craft**
308 Streatham High Road
Streatham
London SW16 3HG
Website: www.artandcraft.london
*Art on the walls, craft beer on the shelves.*

**B Street Deli**
88 Bermondsey Street
SE1 3UB
Telephone: 0207 403 3943
Website: www.bstreetdeli.co.uk
*Your local deli on Bermondsey Street. Fine food epicerie, casual wine bar.*

**Bell & Sons Butchers**
13a Market Place
Bermondsey
London SE16 3UQ
Telephone: 0207 394 1125
Website:
www.bellandsonsbutchers.co.uk
*A modern butchers with classic values, we provide quality meat with wonderful service, 20 years in the making.*

**Brett and Bailey**
Telephone: 020 8144 8414
Website: www.brettandbailey.co.uk
*A South London duo with a growing and loyal fanbase among Crystal Palace market regulars and private clients alike thanks to their knack of making the best of all things baked, sweet, sticky, and delicious.*

**Brisket and Barrel**
123 St Johns Hill
Sevenoaks TN13 3PE
Telephone: 01732 453 934
Website: www.brisketandbarrel.co.uk
*At Brisket and Barrel you can order a choice of hot smoked meat to enjoy in or out, alongside our signature side dishes.*

**Brown & Green**
Crystal Palace
Station Road
London
SE19 2BF
Telephone: 0208 761 6409
Website: www.brownandgreencafe.com
*Five brunch kitchen cafés run by sisters
Laura and Jess Tilli serving up breakfast
and brunch classics with inspired twists
around the Crystal Palace and Sydenham
area. See website for further locations.*

**Canopy Beer Co**
Arch 1127 Bath Factory Estate
41 Norwood Road
London SE24 9AJ
Telephone: 0208 671 9496
Website: www.canopybeer.com
*Brewery and tap room in Herne Hill
with an emphasis on drinkable, accessible
and seasonal beers made with minimal
intervention – no filtration, no finings
and no pasteurisation.*

**Cellar.sw4**
1 Voltaire Rd
London  SW4 6DQ
Telephone: 0203 609 1331
Website: www.cellar-sw4.co.uk
*Wine bar and shop from the people behind
Dvine Cellars in Clapham, specialising
in biodynamic, organic and sustainable
wines.*

**Chadwicks**
109 Balham High Road
Balham
London SW12 9AP
Telephone: 0208 772 1895
Website: www.chadwicksbutchers.com
*Quality family butchers – our meat is
responsibly sourced and British farmed
with provenance.*

**Chadwicks**
106-108 Tooting High Street
Tooting Broadway
London SW17 0RR
Telephone: 0208 672 9852
Website: www.chadwicksbutchers.com
*Quality family butchers – our meat is
responsibly sourced and British farmed
with provenance.*

**Champor-Champor**
62 Weston Street
London SE1 3QJ
Telephone: 0207 403 4600
Website: www.champor-champor.com
*Unique Thai and Malay dining
experience in the heart of London.*

**Chocolates by Eloise Directory**
Telephone: 07985 367325
Website: www.chocolatesbyeloise.co.uk
*Award-winning sister-run chocolatiers
creating the finest Belgian chocolates laced
with contemporary flavours and textures.*

**Christopher's Bakery**
145 Half Moon Lane
North Dulwich
London SE24 9JY
Telephone: 0203 643 6540
Website:
www.christophersbakery.co.uk
*Bakery, delicatessen and café.*

**Comfort & Joy**
9a Church Road
Upper Norwood
London SE19 2TA
Telephone: 07916 262576
Website:
www.comfortandjoycaterers.co.uk
*Using only fresh and home-cooked
ingredients, Comfort & Joy caterers
prepare and deliver food for parties,
events, markets and functions.*

**Constancia**
52 Tanner Street
London SE1 3PH
Telephone: 0207 234 0676
Website: www.constancia.co.uk
*Constancia is an independent, family-run
Argentine grill and steak house, located in
the heart of Bermondsey's former tannery
and leather district.*

**Dugard & Daughters – Butcher and
Larder**
286 Arch
Milkwood Road
Herne Hill
London
SE24 0EZ
Telephone: 0207 733 2608
Website:
www.dugardanddaughters.com
*A family-run butchers specialising in
free-range and rare-breed meats, with a
wonderful emphasis on being a 'one-
stop-shop' for everything needed to make
superb, hearty meals for all the family.*

**D Vine Cellars**
74 Landor Road
London
SW9 9PH
Telephone: 0207 733 2766
Website: www.dvinecellars.com
*D Vine Cellars specialise in handcrafted
organic and biodynamic wine.*

**Elvira's Secret Pantry**
71 Groveland Road
Beckenham BR3 3PX
Telephone: 07817 798650
Website: www.elvirassecretpantry.com
*London-based artisan Italian bakery
specialising in freshly baked products free
from gluten, dairy and yeast.*

**Estate Office Coffee**
1 Drewstead Rd
Streatham
London SW16 1LY
Telephone: 0203 627 0647
Website: www.estateofficecoffee.co.uk
*Independent coffee shop serving locally roasted Allpress coffee, plus artisan-made cakes, pastries, breads and savoury delights.*

**Flock and Herd Butchery**
155 Bellenden Road
Peckham
London SE15 4DH
Telephone: 0207 635 7733
Website: www.flockandherd.com
*Butchery who aim to provide the very best possible quality and range of produce, enabling them to provide customers with the best in taste, service and experience.*

**Flotsam & Jetsam Cafe**
4 Bellevue Parade
Wandsworth Common
London SW17 7EQ
Telephone: 0208 672 7639
Website:
www.flotsamandjetsamcafe.co.uk
*Flotsam & Jetsam is an independently owned Antipodean-style café offering delicious Allpress espresso coffee, all-day brunch and freshly baked pastries, cakes, and slices.*

**Franklins Farm Shop**
155 Lordship Lane
London SE22 8HX
Telephone: 0208 693 3992
Website: www.franklinsrestaurant.com
*Farm shop specialising in seasonal British produce.*

**Franklins Restaurant**
157 Lordship Lane
London SE22 8HX
Telephone: 0208 299 9598
Website: www.franklinsrestaurant.com
*Restaurant serving seasonal British dishes made with Kent farm vegetables and rare-breed meats.*

**The Garrison Public House**
99 Bermondsey Street
London
SE1 3XB
Telephone: 0207 089 9355
Website: www.thegarrison.co.uk
*An award-winning mainstay of South London's thriving food scene, the Garrison offers an ever-changing seasonal menu sourced from local suppliers and British farms and fishermen, serving it up with inspired drinks choices in a welcoming, atmospheric and relaxing environment.*

**Graveney Gin Limited**
Unit 17, Merton Abbey Mills
1929 Building
Watermill Way SW19 2RD
Telephone: 07398 531795
Website: www.graveneygin.co.uk
*Organic/playful/handcrafted/nano-distillery/charity.*

**The Habit Peckham**
67 Peckham road
London SE5 8UH
Telephone: 0207 252 7649
Website: www.thehabitlondon.co.uk
*Committed to bringing a place where families and friends can enjoy great food, wine and local produce, to the neighbourhood.*

**The Habit Nunhead**
60 Nunhead Lane
London SE15 3QE
Telephone:  0207 635 9060
Website: www.thehabitlondon.co.uk
*A modern British bistro, we like keeping it fresh, simple and seasonal.*

**Hayman's Gin**
8A Weir Road
Balham
London SW12 0GT
Telephone: TBC
Website: www.haymansgin.com
*We make award-winning English gin the original way, just as we always have.*

**The Inkspot Brewery Ltd**
The Rookery Barn
40 Streatham Common South
Streatham
London SW16 3BX
Telephone: 0208 679 7322
Website: www.theinkspotbrewery.com
*Two friends, a brewery in a London Edwardian garden; winning hearts and minds with beer.*

**Jensen's Gin**
Bermondsey Gin Ltd.
55 Stanworth Street
London SE1 3NY
Telephone: 0207 237 1500
Website: www.jensensgin.com
*Distilled in Bermondsey, London, Jensen's is gin as it was; Gin as it should be.*

**José Tapas Bar**
104 Bermondsey Street
London SE1 3UB
Website:
www.josepizarro.com/jose-tapas-bar
*Experience a true taste of Spain in our little corner of Bermondsey.*

**LASSCO Brunswick House**

30 Wandsworth Road,
Vauxhall,
London SW8 2LG
Telephone: 0207 394 2100
Website: www.lassco.co.uk

**LASSCO Ropewalk**

37 Maltby Street,
Bermondsey,
London
SE1 3PA
Telephone: 0207 394 8061
Website: www.lassco.co.uk

**London Smoke & Cure**

5 Stoney Lane
London SE19 3BD
Telephone: 07838 838241
Website:
www.londonsmokeandcure.co.uk
*An innovative little smokehouse out to
change your perception of how good food
can get.*

**Olley's Fish Experience**

65-69 Norwood Road
Herne Hill
London SE24 9AA
Telephone:
0208 671 8259/0208 671 5665
Website: www.olleys.info
*Award-winning fish and chip shop and
restaurant, serving MSC-certified fish.*

**Piccalilli Caff**

Surrey Docks Farm
Rotherhithe Street
London SE16 5ET
Telephone: 0207 237 6892
Website: www.piccalillicaff.com
*'Where spooning leads to forking'.*

**Pizarro Restaurant**

194 Bermondsey Street
London SE1 3TQ
Telephone: 0207 378 9455
Website: www.josepizarro.com/
pizarro-restaurant
*Pizarro's critically-acclaimed second
Bermondsey restaurant.*

**Salt + Pickle**

67 Westow Hill
London
SE19 1TS
Website: www.saltandpickle.com
*Cured, pickled and preserved food, proper
beers and boutique wines.*

**Single Directory Co**

Unit 12
The Long Shop
Merton Abbey Mills
London
SW19 2RD
Telephone: 07764 747982
Website: www.singlevariety.co.uk
*An award-winning maker of jams and
preserves, Single Variety Co's products uses
fruit seasonally sourced direct from small
local farmers and they specialise in using
higher fruit and lower sugar contents
than traditional recipes in small batches
to preserve the delicious fresh flavour and
vibrant colour.*

**Tooting Full of Flavour**

Contact Brian Albuquerque,
Tooting Town Centre Manager
Telephone: 0208 682 3658
Twitter @TootingTown
*We have great restaurants, pubs, bars
and cafes, a large concentration of small
independent shops, two thriving indoor
markets and many high-street chain
stores.*

**Trinity / Upstairs at Trinity / Bistro
Union**

4, The Polygon
London
SW4 0JG
Telephone: 0207 622 1199
Website: www.trinityrestaurant.co.uk
*Triumvirate of South London eateries
headed by chef Adam Byatt; the Michelin-
starred Trinity specialises in seasonal
menus serving sophisticated twists on
classical-inspired dishes.*

**The Watch House**

199 Bermondsey St,
London
SE1 3UW
Tel: 0207 407 6431
Website: www.thewatchhouse.com
*A dynamic young company serving
consistently great coffee, hand-prepared
food and accompaniments in iconic and
atmospheric surroundings.*

**The Watch House Tower Bridge**

Cardamom Building
31 Shad Thames
London
SE1 2YR
Telephone: 0207 407 0000
Website: www.thewatchhouse.com
*A dynamic young company serving
consistently great coffee, hand-prepared
food and accompaniments in iconic and
atmospheric surroundings.*

# INDEX

## A

allspice 153
almond 9, 91, 121
apple 17, 21, 23, 27, 135, 161, 177
aubergine 151, 168
avocado 8, 17, 34, 37, 96, 118, 174

## B

bacon 9, 100, 103, 107, 108, 138
baking powder 33, 99, 155
balsamic vinegar 73
banana 10, 96
barbecue 23
basil 9, 121
bay 103, 107, 151, 159, 173
bean 8, 17, 62
beef 23, 24, 46, 49, 50, 66, 69, 70, 75, 79, 100, 103, 118, 156, 159
beef stock 49, 75, 79, 103
beer 14, 18, 21, 23, 42, 45, 104, 115, 132, 182, 184
beetroot 73, 147
belly 27, 108, 138
bicarbonate of soda 45
black pepper 21, 27, 141, 159, 177
bread 10, 13, 24, 31, 37, 58, 61, 70, 79, 88, 92, 96, 104, 162, 177
breadcrumbs 91, 95, 153, 159
brown sugar 13, 31, 45, 121, 161
butter 9, 13, 21, 31, 33, 37, 45, 49, 57, 75, 79, 96, 99, 103, 107, 118, 138, 143, 167, 173, 177
butter beans 21
buttercream 33
buttermilk 99

## C

cake 8, 9, 28, 33, 45, 88, 96, 99, 111, 155
cardamom 31
carrot 9, 95, 107, 137, 173
caster sugar 31, 33, 45, 57, 91, 99, 155, 159, 167, 173
cauliflower 75
cheddar 23, 75, 138
chicken stock 107, 141
chilli 13, 17, 34, 37, 50, 151, 159, 168
chillies 13, 17
chipotle 17
chocolate 8, 10, 45, 54, 57, 66, 143
chorizo 9, 10, 111
chutney 9, 79, 95, 161
cider 9, 17, 107, 159, 162, 177
cinnamon 17, 31, 122, 155, 161
cloves 17, 21, 53, 65, 103, 107, 121, 141, 151, 155, 179
cocktail 117, 125, 155, 168
cocoa 45, 54, 173
coconut 96
cod 9, 111, 144, 168
coffee 4, 9, 10, 38, 50, 58, 88, 92, 118, 132, 174, 184, 185
coriander 9, 17, 65, 122, 147, 151, 159, 173, 179
cornflour 137
courgette 9, 111, 118, 121
cream 8, 9, 45, 53, 143, 167, 173
cream cheese 45
croissant 23
cucumber 115, 159
cumin 17, 65, 69, 108, 151
curry 8, 50, 53, 62, 168
custard 167

## D

dill 159
double cream 143, 173
duck 9, 138, 141, 156

## E

egg 8, 9, 31, 33, 49, 53, 69, 91, 95, 99, 103, 111, 118,
143, 153, 159, 177, 179

## F

falafel 62, 168
fennel 27, 151, 153, 173
feta 96, 151
fillet 111, 156
fish 9, 62, 104, 144, 147, 173
flat leaf parsley 147
flour 28, 31, 33, 45, 49, 53, 61, 65, 69, 75, 91, 99, 103,
107, 111, 153, 155, 167
focaccia 96
fruit 118, 161, 162, 168

## G

gammon 177
garlic 17, 21, 27, 53, 65, 79, 103, 107, 108, 111, 121,
141, 151, 159, 168, 179
gelatine 99
gherkin 23
gin 4, 9, 104, 112, 115, 117, 122, 125, 126, 184
ginger 115, 125, 137, 161
gluten-free 10, 62, 88, 91, 144
goat's cheese 95
goose 8, 21, 75
grapeseed 99
gravy 75, 103
grenadine 125

## H

haddock 144
hake 144
ham 41, 69, 177
herring 144
honey 4, 24, 177

## I

ice cream 9, 143
icing sugar 45

## J

jalapeño 17
juniper 122, 129, 131, 151, 153

## K

kale 141
kidney 9, 21, 24, 103

## L

lamb 8, 46, 50, 70, 73, 100
lard 69
lasagne 9, 121
leek 173
lemon 88, 91, 99, 108, 111, 117, 122, 125, 131, 144,
147, 155, 159, 162, 165, 168, 173, 177, 179
lentil 9
lettuce 23, 147, 159
lime 17, 125, 141, 147
liquorice 122
lobster 9, 173

## M

mace 108
maple 143
marmalade 177
marmite 37
mayonnaise 23, 79, 179
milk 13, 31, 41, 53, 75, 167, 174
mince 179
mustard 24, 75, 95, 107, 159, 173, 177

## N

nutmeg 108, 122

# O

onion 9, 13, 17, 21, 49, 65, 69, 79, 95, 107, 137, 151, 153, 159, 173
onion powder 159
orange 9, 122, 147, 155, 177
oyster 53

# P

panko 153
paprika 17, 69, 103, 111, 151, 153, 159, 179
parsley 65, 141, 147, 151, 177
passata 121
pasta 88
pea 108
pear 9, 161
pepper 13, 17, 21, 23, 27, 37, 41, 49, 53, 65, 69, 75, 79, 103, 107, 108, 111, 137, 141, 147, 153, 159, 177, 179
peppercorn 50
pickled 17, 23, 156, 173
pine nuts 50
pizza 31
plum 21
polenta 88
pomegranate 50
porchetta 8
pork 24, 27, 46, 66, 70, 100, 108, 138, 153, 159
porridge 96
porter 45
potato 50, 168
prosecco 33, 34, 117
puff pastry 49, 95

# R

rack 45
rapeseed 121
raspberries 125, 162
red wine 27, 49, 50, 75, 121, 151
rice 168
ricotta 111
risotto 108
rocket 13, 34, 37, 41
rose 9, 131, 155
rosemary 27, 103, 129
rump 8, 73
rye 37, 58, 61

# S

sage 95
salami 41
salmon 9, 138, 147, 156
salt 13, 17, 21, 27, 31, 33, 37, 41, 49, 57, 61, 65, 69, 70, 73, 75, 99, 103, 111, 137, 138, 141, 147, 153, 159, 161, 168, 173, 177, 179
samphire 108
sausage 9, 24, 62, 92, 95, 111, 153
sea salt 17, 21, 31, 57, 147, 173
sesame 137, 168
shallot 111
shellfish 144
sherry 111
shoulder 108
shrimp 156
smoked 8, 17, 21, 23, 69, 103, 108, 111, 138, 141, 143, 151, 153, 156, 182
sour cream 45
sourdough 8, 13, 34, 58, 61, 79, 96, 118, 174, 177
soy 137
spinach 69
squash 153
star anise 21, 173
steak 24, 66, 183
stock 18, 28, 46, 49, 70, 75, 76, 79, 103, 107, 112, 141, 173
suet 103
sugar 10, 13, 17, 31, 33, 45, 53, 57, 79, 91, 99, 121, 125, 135, 155, 159, 161, 162, 165, 167, 173, 177
sunflower 58, 99, 155
syrup 31, 117, 125, 135, 143, 155

# T

*tarragon 173*
*tea 31, 38, 96, 99*
*thyme 103, 107, 111, 151, 173*
*tofu 9, 50, 137*
*tomato 8, 9, 13, 21, 23, 111, 121, 159, 173, 174*
*tonic water 125*
*treacle 100*
*turkey 24*
*turmeric 8, 53, 159*

# V

*vanilla 45, 99, 155, 167, 173*
*veal 70, 100*
*vegan 10, 50, 62, 88*
*vegetable oil 137*
*vegetarian 50, 62, 79, 168*
*venison 100*
*vinegar 13, 17, 41, 73, 111, 121, 137, 159, 161, 162,*
*        173, 177*
*vodka 33, 135*

# W

*wine 10, 13, 27, 38, 49, 50, 53, 66, 75, 76, 79, 81, 104,*
*        121, 132, 135, 151, 156, 161, 170, 173, 177,*
*        182, 183, 184*
*wine vinegar 13, 121, 161, 173, 177*

# Y

*yeast 31, 88, 183*
*yoghurt 99, 179*

# Other titles in the 'Get Stuck In' series

**The Essex Cook Book** features Thomas Leatherbarrow, The Anchor Riverside, Great Garnetts, Deersbrook Farm, Mayfield Bakery and lots more.
*978-1-910863-25-1*

**The South London Cook Book** features Jose Pizarro, Adam Byatt, The Alma, Piccalilli Caff, Canopy Beer, Inkspot Brewery and lots more.
*978-1-910863-27-5*

**The Bristol Cook Book** features Dean Edwards, Lido, Clifton Sausage, The Ox, and wines from Corks of Cotham plus lots more.
*978-1-910863-14-5*

**The Oxfordshire Cook Book** features Mike North of The Nut Tree Inn, Sudbury House, Jacobs Inn, The Muddy Duck and lots more.
*978-1-910863-08-4*

**The Lancashire Cook Book** features Andrew Nutter of Nutters Restaurant, Bertram's, The Blue Mallard and lots more.
*978-1-910863-09-1*

**The Liverpool Cook Book** features Burnt Truffle, The Art School, Fraîche, Villaggio Cucina and many more.
*978-1-910863-15-2*

**The Sheffield Cook Book - Second Helpings** features Jameson's Tea Rooms, Craft & Dough, The Wortley Arms, The Holt, Grind Café and lots more.
*978-1-910863-16-9*

**The Leeds Cook Book** features The Boxtree, Crafthouse, Stockdales of Yorkshire and lots more.
*978-1-910863-18-3*

**The Cotswolds Cook Book** features David Everitt-Matthias of Champignon Sauvage, Prithvi, Chef's Dozen and lots more.
*978-0-9928981-9-9*

**The Shropshire Cook Book** features Chris Burt of The Peach Tree, Old Downton Lodge, Shrewsbury Market, CSons and lots more.
*978-1-910863-32-9*

**The Norfolk Cook Book** features Richard Bainbridge, Morston Hall, The Duck Inn and lots more.
*978-1-910863-01-5*

**The Lincolnshire Cook Book** features Colin McGurran of Winteringham Fields, TV chef Rachel Green, San Pietro and lots more.
*978-1-910863-05-3*

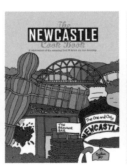

**The Newcastle Cook Book** features David Coulson of Peace & Loaf, Bealim House, Grainger Market, Quilliam Brothers and lots more.
*978-1-910863-04-6*

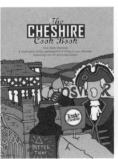

**The Cheshire Cook Book** features Simon Radley of The Chester Grosvenor, The Chef's Table, Great North Pie Co., Harthill Cookery School and lots more.
*978-1-910863-07-7*

**The Leicestershire & Rutland Cook Book** features Tim Hart of Hambleton Hall, John's House, Farndon Fields, Leicester Market, Walter Smith and lots more.
*978-0-9928981-8-2*

*All books in this series are available from Waterstones, Amazon and independent bookshops.*

FIND OUT MORE ABOUT US AT WWW.MEZEPUBLISHING.CO.UK